MEMOIRS OF
SIR LOWRY COLE

MEMOIRS
OF
SIR LOWRY COLE

EDITED BY
MAUD LOWRY COLE
AND
STEPHEN GWYNN

The Naval & Military Press Ltd

Published by

The Naval & Military Press Ltd
Unit 10 Ridgewood Industrial Park,
Uckfield, East Sussex,
TN22 5QE England

Tel: +44 (0) 1825 749494
Fax: +44 (0) 1825 765701

www.naval-military-press.com
www.military-genealogy.com
www.militarymaproom.com

In reprinting in facsimile from the original, any imperfections are inevitably reproduced and the quality may fall short of modern type and cartographic standards.

PREFACE

WHEN Mr. Guedalla was working on his *Life of Wellington*, Sir Lowry Cole's papers were placed at his disposal: and he observed that a book of interest could be made from them. Miss Maud Lowry Cole, acting on the suggestion, went to work, and the present volume is the result. Unhappily she died before the manuscript was quite ready for publication; it was submitted to me and I undertook to do what seemed necessary. In the chapters dealing with the Peninsular War, revision was carried out by my brother, Major-General Sir Charles Gwynn; and Sir Herbert Read, who became Governor of Mauritius just a hundred years after Sir Lowry Cole, kindly reviewed the chapter dealing with that colony. My own part was merely one of technical rearrangement and the addition of a few notes, to help comprehension.

But essentially this book is a memoir of this very distinguished soldier compiled by his granddaughter nearly one hundred and sixty years after Lowry Cole was born.

STEPHEN GWYNN

CONTENTS

CHAPTER I
                                                            PAGE
INTRODUCTORY 1

CHAPTER II
LOWRY COLE AND THE EGYPTIAN CAMPAIGN . . 15

CHAPTER III
MAIDA 33

CHAPTER IV
FIRST EXPERIENCES IN THE PENINSULA . . . 54

CHAPTER V
ALBUERA 68

CHAPTER VI
SALAMANCA 79

CHAPTER VII
THE BATTLES OF THE PYRENEES . . . 95

CHAPTER VIII
THE PEACE OF PARIS 109

CHAPTER IX
THE HUNDRED DAYS 130

CONTENTS

CHAPTER X
AFTER WATERLOO 145

CHAPTER XI
PARIS AFTER THE RESTORATION 164

CHAPTER XII
WITH THE ARMY OF OCCUPATION IN FRANCE . 182

CHAPTER XIII
MAURITIUS 202

CHAPTER XIV
AT THE CAPE OF GOOD HOPE 229

APPENDIX A 253
APPENDIX B 256
APPENDIX C 258

LIST OF ILLUSTRATIONS

Facing page

SIR GALBRAITH LOWRY COLE } . . . 144
LADY FRANCES HARRIS

CATHERINE GERTRUDE HARRIS . . . } 182
HARRIET, DAUGHTER OF SIR GEORGE AMYAND, BART.

CHAPTER I

INTRODUCTORY

It has always been a matter of pride to the Cole family that their ancestor was one of King James's men—undertakers, as they were called—who helped to make Ulster a prosperous and well-to-do province.

Among others, William Cole, of a good Devonshire family, obtained a grant of land which included the town and castle of Enniskillen, situated on an island in Lough Erne. Formerly a stronghold of the rebel Tyrconnell clans, it had lately been garrisoned by English soldiers, but these had not been able to hold it against the famous Hugh O'Donnell and his fleet of long ships who terrorised all the dwellers on Lough Erne.

William Cole's grant carried with it certain conditions. He undertook to construct the town of Enniskillen. For its defence and decency he was required to set apart "a convenient place for a church to be built and a cemetery for the same, a convenient place for a gaol or prison for the safe keeping of prisoners and other malefactors within the bounds of the county of Fermanagh; also a piece of ground for a public school, together with a court and garden to the said school adjoining".

The grant was made in 1612, and a few months later a Charter was conferred on the town constituting it a Borough, having a Corporation of fourteen members of which William Cole was Provost.

In 1617 he was knighted, and in the Parliament of 1639 represented the County. When the great rebellion of the native Irish broke out in 1641 he was governor of the town of Enniskillen, and raised in its defence most of the forces in Fermanagh and preserved that part of the country from the dangers that threatened it.

From that time forth Enniskillen was the refuge and centre of the Protestant inhabitants of the North. The fact that in the native Irish they had a bitter, relentless foe welded the English settlers more closely together, and the religious antagonism between the parties made a mutual drawing together impossible. The settlers held their power grimly: though they despised their enemies, they also feared them; and for a hundred years there was no peace and very little pity.

Early in the eighteenth century Sir John Cole, head of the family, moved out into the country to the woods and mountains ten miles from Enniskillen and there built a house which he named Florence Court after his wife, the daughter of Sir Bourchier Wrey of Trebitch in Cornwall. It has been the home of the family ever since.

John Cole, grandson of the man who built Florence Court, was created Baron Mount Florence of Florence Court in 1760. His son, William Willoughby, born in 1736, was created Viscount Enniskillen in 1776 and Earl of Enniskillen in 1789. He married Anne, daughter of Galbraith Lowry Corry, afterwards Earl of Belmore, and had a large family. Of

INTRODUCTORY

these, four sons and four daughters lived to grow up.

Galbraith Lowry Cole, the subject of this memoir, was William Cole's second son.

But it is not the history of an individual that I propose to write so much as that of his family and his friends as described by themselves in their letters and in his own. To read the various records preserved through several generations is to observe certain characteristics which show more or less distinctly in most of the Coles.

They were energetic, masterful men, who interested themselves in local and public affairs; capable leaders and as such looked up to and respected by their neighbours; loving sport and country pursuits but with only a tepid interest in literature and art; careless about money, yet acutely aware of the need of it to make life pleasant; having a high sense of honour, but also a high temper and lack of patience and caution.

It has been remarked that the lives of the larger number of well-to-do families in England were little affected by the upheaval of the French Revolution and the Napoleonic wars. The calm routine of existence in country parts flowed on, its monotony merely broken by a visit to Bath or London. It was not so in Ireland. There peace and security were as ever impossible, the last twenty years of the eighteenth century being some of the most troubled in Irish annals.

It was during these years that Lowry Cole and his brothers and sisters grew up. The attempted landing of the French in Bantry Bay, the calling out of the militia to defend the country, followed by the rebellion of the native Irish, which culminated in the battle of Vinegar Hill, events with which they were closely connected, made a stormy background for their youthful days. Lord Enniskillen, along with his neighbours, Lord Tyrone, the Marquis of Abercorn and many others, raised bodies of militia which they provided, and officered with their sons. And while his father and brother were actively employed against the rebels in Ulster and Leinster, Lowry was serving on Lord Cornwallis' staff and was present at the Battle of Vinegar Hill.

Lord Enniskillen had large properties both in the North and in Waterford, but, like many Irish landlords, he was improvident and far too ready to spend money on elections—on one occasion pouring out large sums on a contest for the County with a man of the same politics as himself. He had an expensive family—four sons to educate and start in professions, four daughters to dower. No wonder there are constant allusions in the family letters to the lack of money. At the same time neither the troubled state of the country nor straitened means seem to have interfered with the enjoyment of these young people. They hunted, they attended gaieties in Dublin, and when, after the Act of Union, that city lost its prestige and attractions, they went to London or to Paris and the Continent. Young Lowry Cole added to these enjoyments his profession and his duties as a member of parliament; for he represented Fermanagh in the Irish parliament and afterwards at Westminster.

Lowry Cole was born at Florence Court, May 1st, 1772; went to school at Armagh and Portarlington

INTRODUCTORY

and entered the army at the age of fifteen as cornet in the 12th Light Dragoons. He completed his education at the University of Stuttgart, where he studied the art of war for two years, 1790-92, as was customary for English officers. At this time there were no military colleges in England where officers could study the theory of war, no manœuvres where they could learn their all-important duties in the field. Thus Wellington, after leaving Eton, was sent to the military college at Angers; Moore was taught drill and fortification in Germany and Switzerland; Craig, who commanded the expedition to the Mediterranean in 1805 and on whose staff Lowry served, had also studied a considerable time abroad. During this period of study his promotion was advanced with the rapidity proper for a peer's son with an indulgent father. A lieutenancy in the 5th Dragoon Guards was bought for him in 1791, and in 1792 he exchanged into the 70th Regiment as captain.

Lowry Cole also combined some pleasant travel with his studies, for he joined his elder brother, Viscount Cole, and passed some time with him in Vienna.

Lord Cole had been previously on a tour through Italy, staying at Rome, Florence and Naples, where he was made much of in the cosmopolitan society of those cities, being exceedingly handsome, according to a portrait painted at this time. Especially he had made great friends with Lord and Lady Malmesbury. Malmesbury, a leading English diplomat of that time, had begun his successes when sent on a mission to the Empress Catherine. The good looks and charm of Mr. Harris—as he then was—

detached Catherine from the influence of the French ambassador; so Mr. Harris became Sir James and remained in St. Petersburg, except for special missions—one of which sent him to escort Caroline of Brunswick on her wedding journey to England. Finally he was made Lord Malmesbury. In 1792 he was on the Continent only for his pleasure. His very lively lady wrote from Florence on April 21st, 1792, to the handsome young Irishman, whom she had fitted with the obvious nickname of His Majesty King Cole. She details the news from England, as found in a great many letters on her arrival at Florence, which she thought would be "acceptable in Sicily"—where he had gone from Rome :

"The Prince has discarded Mrs. Crouch[1] and now never leaves Mrs. Fitzherbert a minute. There was a dreadful scene at the opera. He came into the box and found Lascelles and Mon^r. de Noailles (whom he detests) there. He had already desired they might never enter it, and he flew into such a rage that people opposite heard what he said. She cried, and at last went out before the opera was over with Bill Pigott. The Prince was certainly too angry, but Lascelles was likewise much to blame to be in a place he was forbidden to enter, and must

[1] A handsome singer who appeared first on the stage as Miss Phillips. In 1792, being separated from her husband, she was living in Pall Mall with Michael Kelly, another singer. According to Huish (*Memoirs of George IV*) the Prince spent £10,000 on her, in addition to jewels for which he ran up a bill of £5000—an item which greatly angered George III. He also settled £1500 a year on her, but when his debts were revised previous to his marriage, this annuity was disallowed because "no valuable consideration had been given for it". She died in 1805.

INTRODUCTORY

have very little pride to do so. However, it's all made up, I believe, but he is very much *awake* still. He has sold all his race horses. . . .

"You know the slave-trade bill[1] was brought on and was carried upon Dundas's motion of the addition of the word 'gradually' before 'abolished', by 193 to 125. If the question had been put on the original motion, it would have been negatived by a great majority. This went to an immediate abolition of the slave trade and was vehemently supported both by Pitt and Fox, the former for the sake of his character as a virtuous young man, the latter, I guess from the fear of being sold *as a negroe*! It's a vile thing and will probably produce the most fatal effects in the islands. The accounts from S. Domingo are said to be worse than ever. . . .

"The King of Sweden[2] has been assassinated at a masquerade, but is alive though not out of danger. He had an anonymous letter to caution him against going to the ball, but did not attend to it. A man came up and fired into his side with a pistol loaded with one round ball, one ragged one and mitraille besides. He managed to escape in the crowd. The King behaved with great presence of mind and gave all the necessary orders, appointed a regency and commanded the gates of the city to be shut. The assassin was soon taken and confessed the crime. He said he was an officer who had formerly been broke and banished, that the King had pardoned him but that, having since lost a lawsuit unjustly, he had determined on this vile deed, and

[1] This was introduced by Wilberforce. The date fixed for abolition was 1796. But the House of Lords held up the proposal.
[2] Gustavus III succumbed to his wound.

that forty persons of the highest rank were concerned in the conspiracy. Many of these are already arrested. It's a horrid story, but what is not horrid just now!"

Naturally everything was horrid, these years after the French Revolution, when the Terror was in full swing. But England was not yet involved in the struggle; Lowry Cole could still study war academically at Stuttgart, and Lady Malmesbury still enjoy her life abroad. She wrote again from Florence on May 4th, 1792:

"Here we are still and I am only sorry we are not to stay a month longer, for I am quite charmed with this place. But I no longer depend on myself for Lord Malmesbury was obliged by business to go home immediately, and went off last Sunday.

"I never saw any country so beautiful. The verdure is quite divine. And it is the beauty of spring with the hottest summer weather. . . .

"I had the oddest letter in the world from Mackinnon. Quite unprovoked, he says: 'I had the good fortune to come from Rome with Lord Cole, and I was highly pleased with his manly spirit and his generous sentiments, which may be seen on his face'. Now what do you say to that, Your Majesty?

"I think you will be finely melted in Sicily if you are as hot in proportion as we are.

"The next time you write direct to me at Mon^r. Bontemps, Banquier à Genève. We shall be the 11th at Milan and what's to become of all of us I cannot tell you. You know that war is actually declared by France to the King of Hungary and probably by

INTRODUCTORY

this time to the King of Sardinia, so we must expect all sorts of adventures on the frontiers of Savoy.

"This country is in a state of alarm and thinks Leghorn will be taken in a minute. The report is that two French ships of the line are actually gone to bully Naples! So much for Italy.

"I have very little news from England. . . . The old Duchess of Bedford is very ill and very much afraid of being murdered by Mrs. Fitzherbert *from jealousy*. . . .

"We expect to meet Lord Dalkeith at Milan. I don't know whether all this warlike news may not alter his and everybody's plans, for I conclude you will all wish to have a peep at it. If so, I think we may still have a chance of meeting somewhere before I get to England.

"Adieu, my dear King Cole. . . . Que Dieu vous aye dans sa sainte et digne garde.

"Yours ever,
"H. M. M^y."

Again from Spa on August 10th, 1792:

"I found your letter here when I arrived a few days ago. You are the best of Kings and as such I revere you, although you tell me I *am out of my senses for being here*. You would think so much more if you were to see Spa this year—it is the Temple of Ennui! Not a soul of my acquaintance and scarcely any English. I don't think my patience will last a considerable length of time, especially as Mr. Ellis is still more bored than I am and bears it *like a man*. N.B. with the greatest impatience.

"I have excused Lord Malmesbury the journey, though he very handsomely offered to come.

"I am very happy to hear I shall pay my court to Your Majesty in December. But in case I am not in London, I trust you will descend from your throne and condescend to visit your subjects at Brookwood Park.

"I am sorry to hear such bad accounts of my drawings, but I hope you are fastidious.

"All the world is going to Italy next winter and I was on the point of being seduced to return there by Lady Palmerston, who you will know some time or other, as she is my dear friend and one of the pleasantest women in the world. . . .

"We are expecting every day great news, and so high are our expectations raised that what would have made the whole world shudder four years ago would be despised now as a trifle. To-morrow or perhaps to-night the Prussians sleep on French soil and I fancy very few people of that nation will do so besides them. How can you be stupefying yourself at Vienna in such a moment? . . .

"Adieu, my dear Lord Cole. . . .

"Direct to me Spring Gardens, London.

"Yours ever,

"H. M. MALMESBURY"

But this light-hearted dallying on the Continent was brought to an end by the declaration of war between France and England in 1793. This found Lord Cole at Vienna with his brother and brought them both home to serious duties. While Lord Cole returned to Ireland and his usual occupations, Lowry Cole began his active career as a soldier. A

INTRODUCTORY

new step was bought for him and he was gazetted major in the 86th Regiment in 1793, when he was only twenty-one. The 86th being in the West Indies, he was on his way to join it when he fell in with the expedition despatched in that year against the French West Indies, joined it as a volunteer, saw the taking of Martinique and afterwards of Guadeloupe, and was attached as A.D.C. to Sir Charles Grey, who commanded the military force.

He was next promoted Lieut.-Colonel in Ward's Regiment of Foot and from this exchanged into the Coldstream Guards. There is no use blinking the fact that up to a certain point Lowry Cole bought his way. Beyond that, he fought it up, if ever a man did. But in those aristocratic days rapid promotion was possible only to the well-born who were also wealthy. The Napiers, closely connected with both Pitt and Fox, rose slowly, because steps were bought over their heads. Lowry Cole's career was one of the best cases to justify a bad system.

Meanwhile the third son, William Cole, was being pushed ahead with the same rapidity. He is prominent in the letters and in managing the family affairs, living much at Florence Court. But though he had the Deanery of Waterford as well as a small living in a remote part of Ireland, he does not seem to have been tied by his duties, and took part in the gaieties of Dublin and London.

He evidently tried to act as mentor to his youngest brother, Arthur, who would have liked to be a soldier but was obliged to resign himself to the life of a cadet in the East India Company. It led to prosperity, but involved in those days exile and separation from all he loved best.

Lord Enniskillen's eldest daughter, Lady Sarah, married in 1790 Owen Wynne of Haslewood, near Sligo, a prosperous country gentleman much interested in agriculture. The second, Elizabeth Anne, who inherited her mother's beauty, was *petite*, with a lovely *riant* face framed in nut-brown hair. She married in 1788 Richard Magenis, Lieut.-Colonel in the Fermanagh Militia and M.P. for the Borough of Enniskillen. He was a handsome spendthrift and they had a stormy, difficult married life. She was much oppressed by the cares of her numerous family and lack of means. But in times of stress the doors of Florence Court were always open to receive her and her children and even to bolster up her husband.

The third sister, Florence, married in 1797 Blayney Balfour of Townley Hall, Drogheda, a man of substance and fine property, which, however, he reduced considerably by turning the public road so as not to cross his park, and by building an Italian palace of noble proportions on the banks of the Boyne. She was evidently the favourite sister and correspondent of her brothers, continuing all through life to be their intimate friend and confidante, though with a numerous family and many interests to occupy her.

There remains the youngest of the family, Henrietta, who was unmarried at the time of her parents' death. She was considered the handsomest of that handsome family. Dublin gaieties—after the Union—were not thought good enough for her, even though the Lord Lieutenant and his wife

INTRODUCTORY

specially favoured her. A London season was hoped for, either under the wing of her sister, Lady Florence Balfour, or of Lady Carhampton, a family friend.

Returning now to the main subject, apprehensions of a French invasion were sharply felt in Ireland, and Lowry Cole went over to join Lord Carhampton's staff as A.D.C. In that capacity he received a letter dated January 6th, 1797, from Captain Robert Crawford, giving full details of the episode when part of an expedition, sent out under Hoche, reached the coast of Cork without its commander and lay in Bantry Bay for close on a fortnight before Grouchy, senior in command, decided to retreat. This will be found in Appendix A.

From another official document, quoted in Appendix B, May 27th, 1798, it would appear that Lowry Cole was in command of a mixed body, some thirty of the 5th Dragoons, as many more yeomanry from Kells, and two hundred of the Cork City Militia, sent to put down the assembly of insurgents reported at Tara Hill in Meath. Lord Enniskillen with his militia from Enniskillen was in the same area. It should be noted, since Lake, who was in command of the operations during that summer, acquired a name for butchery, that careful control of the troops is enjoined by his order.

At the final encounter in Wexford, which had become the main centre of revolt, Lowry Cole was present and received his first wound during the battle of Vinegar Hill.

Seats in Parliament, like steps in military rank,

were not acquired in those times without expenditure of money; but merit helped, and there can be no doubt that Lowry Cole's service at Vinegar Hill commended him to the electors when he was returned in 1798 as member for County Fermanagh in the Irish Parliament. Also there can be no doubt that Lord Enniskillen had to dip again into his pocket to further the fortunes of this well-provided young man who was at twenty-six Lieut.-Colonel and member of Parliament. He was thus chosen just in time to give his vote for the Legislative Union. Votes for that measure did not go unrewarded, and in January 1801 he was gazetted Colonel in the Army.

But before this, the scene had shifted to more glorious theatres of war; and he was ordered to join the Mediterranean forces at Malta which were under Sir Ralph Abercromby's command.

CHAPTER II

LOWRY COLE AND THE EGYPTIAN CAMPAIGN

In 1797 Bonaparte convinced the Directory that the best way to ruin England would be to occupy Egypt and so threaten her commerce in the Mediterranean and eventually perhaps her dominion in the East. They listened to his arguments, and with their permission and a strong Fleet conveying 40,000 of his best troops, he set out on his adventure. By the narrowest chance he had the luck to escape the British squadron under Nelson.

He landed at Alexandria and defeated the Turks at the Battle of the Pyramids—and all was going successfully when Nelson, who had been cruising about in search of the French for some time in vain, discovered their ships in the harbour of Alexandria, attacked them and completely destroyed them in the Battle of the Nile on August 1st, 1798.

The French army was completely cut off from Europe. The Porte now declared war, and Napoleon determined to attack the Turks by land.

In 1799 he marched into Syria, but the Turks put up such a good defence at Acre—helped by Sir Sidney Smith and his ships—that Napoleon was obliged to retreat. His army regained Cairo after terrible suffering and loss, and without their Commander. He himself, on receiving important news from Paris, secretly deserted them, managed once more to elude the British fleet, and reached Paris in October.

As no English Government could allow Egypt to be occupied by the French, Sir Ralph Abercromby, who commanded the troops in the Mediterranean, was ordered to assemble an expeditionary force at Malta and attack the French on the shore side. Assisted by Sir John Moore he had for months been forming troops and collecting supplies to this end. An Anglo-Indian force under Sir David Baird was to land at Kosseir on the Red Sea, march across the desert into Upper Egypt, descend the Nile, and take the French in the rear.

The Turks were also to combine with the British; but Moore, whom Abercromby sent to confer with the Grand Vizier at Jaffa, gave such a bad report of their organisation that his chief realised it would be useless to rely on help from them.

He was also very badly provided with money, horses and other equipment for his campaign. Even information about Egypt, such as landing-places or maps, was lacking in his instructions. After sailing from Malta he had to land at the Bay of Marmorice in Asia Minor to pick up the horses he required. To pay for them he had to borrow money from some of his well-to-do officers.

Eventually the landing in Egypt had to be made without Baird's contingent or any help from the Turks. He received information of the arrival of two French frigates with reinforcements, and then determined to wait no longer.

Abercromby landed his troops in Aboukir Bay and drove the French from the Peninsula. A few days later the Battle of Alexandria was fought.

THE EGYPTIAN CAMPAIGN

Victory remained with the British, but their gallant leader was mortally wounded and died a few days later. General Hely-Hutchinson became Commander-in-Chief.

These two decisive actions of the war—on the 13th and 21st of March—had been fought and won before Lowry Cole arrived in Egypt. While still on the way, he wrote to his sister Lady Florence Balfour:

Malta, *June 22nd*, 1801
"MY DEAREST FLORENCE,   Just going to Egypt

I arrived here the second of the month after as disagreeable a passage of six days as I ever experienced.

I was agreeably disappointed on my arrival to find that I had permission to follow the army to Egypt; General Villette having been kind enough to obtain this from Sir Ralph Abercromby, knowing I should wish it.

The army consists of 18000 men and are arrived safe at Marmorice Bay. They expected to commence operations the latter end of this month. I hope I shall get in time. What situation I shall be in I do not know but I hope an active one. Meade and I expect to sail very soon. He is to be with Craddock. . . .

This is a most magnificent town and harbour and the fortifications are astonishing, all well cut out of the rock. No expense seems to have been spared to make it impregnable and in our hands I should think it will be so.

It is within a few hours of Sicily. I should not dislike it as quarters, as you can live very comfortably on your pay, which it is not possible to do in England or Ireland.

General Villette remains here as second in command. I am sorry to part with him as I never met a more gentlemanlike man, and nothing can be more civil than he has been to me."

Cole was at this time acting as Lieut.-Colonel in Villette's regiment, a corps of Albanians formed for service in the Mediterranean.

William Anne Villette was of Huguenot stock separated from France by the Edict of Nantes. He had distinguished himself at the siege of Toulon and at the conquest of Corsica in 1794. He governed Malta from 1801 to 1807. Malta had only been in the possession of the British for a little more than a year. Napoleon had seized it from the Knights of Malta when he was on his way to Egypt in 1798, or rather they had relinquished it without a struggle into his hands. The British occupied it a short time later.

From Lowry Cole's Diary we find that his regiment proceeded in July to join the main body. He himself was appointed Military Secretary to General Hely Hutchinson, now Commander-in-Chief of the Expeditionary force. Hutchinson, it should be remarked, belonged like Cole to the Anglo-Irish aristocracy, who always gave each other a helping hand.

The Diary reads as follows:

17th July. Saw Alexandria and anchored in Aboukir Bay.

THE EGYPTIAN CAMPAIGN

20th July. Landed and encamped on the East side of Alexandria.
10th August. Changed our plan of encampment. Attacked and beat the French.
18th August. Encamped nearer the enemy.
19th. The French fired a number of shott, many of which were made of brass.
22nd. We embarked and went to the Westward of Alexandria, arriving in five hours.
The Fort Marabout taken.
Laying on our arms without tents baggage or water.
25th. Got our tents and erected a Battery. Enemy throw shott and shell into our tents.
At night attacked and beat the French, and took 8 Officers prisoner and some more.
26th. An Armistice took place for three days.
29th. The flags of truce still fly.
30th. Articles of Capitulation of Alexandria signed between General the Honble Sir John Hely Hutchinson and General Menon the same day.

Operations had proved much more arduous than would appear from this meagre account. The march across the peninsula to attack the Western front of Alexandria was short but very full of obstacles. The guns and transport had to be dragged first over heavy sand, then across a range of hills pitted with enormous quarries through which it was most difficult to make a way. There were several days' hard fighting in which the troops particularly distinguished themselves before Alexandria capitulated, and on September 3rd, 1801, the Grenadiers of the army with drums beating and colours flying took formal possession of the city.

As soon as transport could be provided, the French were marched to the ships and despatched to France, and with their departure the British Expeditionary Force was broken up. Part remained in Egypt till the Turks were ready to reoccupy it; the remainder were quartered at the various stations in the Mediterranean, such as Minorca, Elba and Malta.

On November 15th, Colonel Lowry Cole embarked at Alexandria on board H.M. *Regulus* and arrived at Malta on December 5th, thence reaching England in January 1802.

Napoleon, now First Consul, made peace with England in 1802, but this was broken in 1803.

Until 1805 Lowry Cole was in England and divided his time between his parliamentary and regimental duties, with short visits to his family, which in that time suffered heavy changes. A grouping of the correspondence will show these and also illustrate the period.

In 1801 the youngest son, Arthur, sailed for India, where he landed on July 26th after a voyage of almost four months. While he was still on the seas, his brother, Dean Cole, wrote to him from the house of their sister Lady Sarah Wynne on Lough Gill near Sligo. The Dean, whose looks had earned him a flattering nickname, "the Beauty of Holiness", was, as will be seen, a man of fashion.

"MY DEAR ARTHUR,
      I was much disappointed at not being able

THE EGYPTIAN CAMPAIGN

to see you before you sailed, but as parting from friends is always unpleasant, perhaps it has happened for the best!

I remained in London much longer than I at first intended as I found it very pleasant when I became acquainted. Lady Carhampton and Darnley got me asked everywhere I wished.

A number of Irish came over after you left. The ladies were but little taken notice of, unless such as had English connexions, so that it is probable they will be satisfied in future with their own country. Some of them were not a little disappointed. Altho' they were admired when they happened to be out, yet few of the Englishmen took any notice of them, and not one of them has got an husband there. . . .

Cole and I went to Mr. Byng's to the Brocket Hall races, where we had a pleasant party. The Prince was there making fierce love to Mrs. Fitzherbert who is very ugly. . . .

August 23rd.—I deferred writing any more for some time. You, my dear fellow, are, I hope, by this time nearly at the end of your tedious voyage. God grant it may prove a successful voyage and that you may come over to us as rich and as happy as all your friends wish you! . . .

I fear from every account that I have had that you will find India very uncomfortable for a few years, but as you were sensible of your situation before you went out, and are not of a desponding disposition, I hope you will make the best of it, especially when you consider how little real happiness can be expected in this world and how particularly disagreeable the position of younger sons of noblemen is here.

Born with the same ideas, introduced into the same society and unfortunately endowed with the same passions as their elders, they naturally are induced to give way to those feelings which in the end become ruin to them.

For as in this world everything gives way to wealth, they have but little chance of success when that comes in competition with them. You will have but little opportunity of feeling this misfortune. Happy would it have been for me could I say the same! And the more so as from my profession it will be necessary for me to marry, and as yet I see no chance of it.

I was in great hopes that Cole would have formed some connexion in England that would have induced him to marry, but I think he is less likely than ever. He was more taken notice of than any Irishman and I believe than most Englishmen, as he had two or three invitations every day to dinner. I feared he was growing too fond of it, but he has returned to Ireland as great a Pat as ever!

We have had several letters from Lowry. He was fortunate in being appointed Aide-de-Camp to Gen[l]. Hutchinson, who now commands since the death of Sir Ralph. He has, poor fellow, escaped the first desperate actions, and from what I hear there never were more gallant actions heard of! They have raised the name of the British soldier once more, and have proved to us that we are equal to them [the French] at any time, notwithstanding all their gasconade!

As you hear everything from Egypt by the Red Sea, I shall not say much on the subject. Only we have just heard that Cairo has surrendered, and that the whole country is expected now to be ours. . . .

Should you find it necessary to have any more letters, write to me, or if you want money or anything else I can procure. Altho' you are sometimes ceremonious in that particular, I am sure you will no longer be so with

Your ever affec^{te}

Beltrim Castle   W. W. C."

Next comes a letter from Arthur Cole to his father, Lord Enniskillen, dated August 10th, 1801. Though the career arranged for him was not congenial to his taste, nor by the standard of the time acceptable for a peer's son, he entered on it well forwarded. The day of his arrival he delivered letters of introduction to Lord Clive and dined with him that same evening.

"I also", he wrote to his father, "called on Mr. Webbe[1] (otherwise the Billy Pitt of India) to whom Lord Hobart gave me a letter.

"He very condescendingly received me, which is reckoned a great honour from him, and told me he was very sorry it was not in his power to offer me a bed, as he himself was living with Lord Clive. But that there were positive orders for every Madras writer to proceed to the College at Calcutta to learn the language, and that the sooner I went on the better.

[1] Josiah Webbe (who by an omission is not in the *D.N.B.*) had been appointed Chief Secretary to the Indian Government—the first holder of that office. The Duke of Wellington described him as "one of the ablest men I ever knew, and what is more, one of the most honest".

"I asked him if it were possible for me to avoid going, but he said the order was so peremptory that Lord Clive could not take it upon himself to allow any young man to remain here.

"By going to Bengal our allowances are doubled, so that our pay will be nearly £500 a year, which is equal to any employment we could hold here during our writership. And after remaining three years at College we are qualified to hold any situation on this establishment.

"The young writers of last year who went there, I am told, complain very much of the strictness of the institution, and also of the expense they are put to by being obliged to go into the volunteer Cavalry Corps, which, unless I am absolutely forced to enter, I shall have nothing to say to. For it would certainly be unpleasant as well as expensive, and call me from what I wish to attend to more. Besides I know I am too fond of it. . . .

"I have met with every civility and have not had a day without an invitation to dine out.

"Lord Clive has been so good as to offer me any money I should want, and Mr. Chase, who came out in the same ship with me, told me he would advance me any sum I should ask for, but of course, as long as I have friends at home, I shall never put myself under obligation to strangers. At present I have enough, and at Calcutta if I want any I can draw for it.

"Now, my dear Sir, I have exhausted my little stock of information. I can only add that I hope to show you that my future conduct will equal my promises. Indeed it will be my only means of returning to you independent. And having so much at stake, I hope, will make me exert myself more in Wellesley College (so-called by Lord Mornington) than I did at Trinity.

"Your affec^{ate} and dutiful son,
"ARTHUR H. J. COLE"

A letter from his mother to this Indian exile gives detail of the family.

Augt. ye 4th, 1802
(Received *June 5th*, 1803)

"The happiness I experienced on getting a letter from you, my dearly beloved child, yesterday dated ye 28th Feby. is only to be conceived by yourself, who feel so much on not hearing from those you love. Add to that what a mother's feeling must be separated from a child so dear without a hope of ever seeing you again, being now too old to expect to live till it may please God for your return.

But I have ever through life put my only trust in God—to prosper you, and if you are well and happy, though ever so far from me, I shall be content and thankful.

First then your Father and I are here and well in spite of bad weather—a total wretched season. . . . Cole just returned to Fermanagh to be chaired with his colleague young Archdall for the county. He found all his steady friends such as Erne and Caldwell, etc. were so much more attached to Archdall than Brooke that to prevent a contest he joined him, and it turned out that even Lord Ely gave him both his votes. . . .

Our dear Lowry returned in January [from Malta] perfectly well. He and Willie went in March to London. From that they have since gone to Paris. They are now, I hear, returned to Dublin and are hourly expected at Florence Court to our races that commence next Monday, ye 8th. . . .

August ye 7th.—I was interrupted by the arrival of your dear brother Lowry, who came to Florence Court on Wednesday and stayed the day after to see me, and is gone again this morning. . . .

As to publick news I have none. You have already heard of Peace which has infused universal joy. I am not pollitician enough to know much about it.

Dublin was uncommonly gay this spring. All the Unionists strove to prevent people from going to live in England by giving Balls and Masquerades.

Lord and Lady Hardwicke were very much liked as Lord and Lady Lieutenant. They gave a number of private entertainments to which Henrietta was always asked.

All the men of fortune are going or gone to England. I hear most of those who voted for the Union are now sorry for it. Government have used all their influence to stop contested elections. There have not been many, few people being able to go and live in England or bear the expense of moving every winter. Jimmy H. gave up Donegall. It was literally going a-begging. There are no less than four of the young Latouches[1] returned for those counties and the City of Dublin, out of which they have turned poor Dr. George Ogle. But you see it is money, money does all everywhere!

Adieu, my beloved child. May God Almighty keep you steady in the principles of virtue and

[1] A family of bankers of French Huguenot stock.

religion. May you never be led to do a wrong action to God or to your fellow creatures, let the profit be ever so great to yourself. Your Father bids me say he has written to you thrice this year. Now to God who governs everything I commit you and remain
Your attached Mother,
A. ENNISKILLEN"

That must have been one of the last letters that came to anyone from Lady Enniskillen; for on October 20th Dean Cole wrote to his brother Arthur:

"You must by this time have heard of my poor dear Mother's death.... My Father, as I expected, was much shocked at first, but having that easy kind of disposition it is now totally worn off.... He talks sometimes of keeping house at Florence Court until the Rusty [his youngest daughter, Henrietta] is married. At other times he says he would like to go abroad.

"God grant he may not think of marrying. That indeed would be a melancholy event for his family, who are already poor enough.

"I had expected that before this Cole would have married. At present I see not the smallest chance of it—and Lowry since that love affair with Kitty Pakenham seems like a burnt child to fear the fire and not to have any wish to hazard his happiness by paying attention to any of them....

"You must be happy to hear that Cole came in without any expense for the County. His affairs required it much.

"I have persuaded Lowry to take chambers. He

is going on very well, but is rather slow. Apropos! you have never written the long-promised letter to Lowry. As he is ceremonious, you had better write to him. But never make any apologies. Write as if you had written before.

"He is very well but not attached yet; unless the war begins again I fear he will wait long."

In other words, Colonel Lowry Cole was on half-pay—though he did not have long to wait.

There are many allusions to "Kitty Pakenham", who in the opinion of his family played fast and loose with his affections. She was to make a greatly more illustrious alliance; but as the Duchess of Wellington, she perhaps more than atoned for whatever her inconstancy may have inflicted on Lowry Cole.

Lord Enniskillen also wrote to Arthur Cole in December 1803, with lamentation about "the best of wives and the best of mothers".

"I have done everything your dear Mother wished. I have made Henrietta mistress of the house and shall keep, please God, whilst I live a house for my children, where I hope we shall often meet as usual during that time which it shall please God to allow me to remain here. . . .

"Lowry is with us, hearty and well, but is now hunting at French Park with his brother William."

Five months later, Lord Enniskillen was dead also. Lord Cole succeeding to the peerage, the seat for County Fermanagh was vacant: Dean Cole on

THE EGYPTIAN CAMPAIGN

July 1st, 1803, tells his Indian brother how it was kept in the family.

Townley Hall,
July 1st, 1803
(Recd. *July 8th*, 1804)

"My dear Arthur,

Since the dissolution of my dear Parent, my mind has been wholly occupied with that event and with the idea of a dreadful contest which was likely to ensue on account of the dreadful desertion of young Colonel Archdall. We have, thank God, defeated their schemes and I am happy in having it in my power to say that Lowry was returned without opposition last Monday sennight. Almost all our friends were steady except Lord Lanesborough.

We had the Colonel chaired in great form, covered with orange and blue. He entered into the canvass with great spirit.

My poor Father left him very comfortably. He has given him £4,000 which, added to the price of the Borough, gives him £10,000, besides an estate worth £230 per annum. The Duke of York has also given him a company in the Guards supposed to be worth above £600 per ann. So he is well off as a younger son.

He has left Bess [Lady E. Magenis] £1,000, which makes her fortune £7,000. He has left £6,000 to Rusty [Lady Henrietta Cole], to you £4,000 with a charge of £2,000, I *believe*, on the English property when it comes into Cole's [Lord Cole] hands, to me £4,000 with a similar charge of £1,000.

I have but little news. This year I have not been much in the world. Lowry and I were on our road to England when we heard of my Father's illness. At present I think of going with Bal [his brother-in-law, Mr. Balfour] and Florence there for a few months. . . .

Lowry is expected here on Friday on his way to attend Parliament and his regiment. Don't be surprised if you hear that Rusty will be married to Lord Carrick's son. He seems to have a penchant for her, and *entre nous* her Ladyship is rather smitten. Belmore [his Uncle, Lord Belmore] and Juliana [Lady B.] seem anxious for it. . . .

Kitty [Lady Catherine Pakenham] is at Cheltenham. I am beginning to think she wishes to bring on the subject again with Lowry, but he fights shy. She will deserve it as she treated him cruelly. . . .

Rusty was disappointed at not going this winter to Lady Carhampton. As Eliza Lutterel will go out next year, Lady C. don't seem to wish to have her, which perhaps may be happy for her in the future. It is possible she might marry then, which would separate her from her friends and place her in a dangerous situation. Few places are more enticing for a young woman and it is the fashion there for men so much to neglect their wives! . . . Write to me soon.

Your ever attached,
W. W. COLE"

The same to the same, from Florence Court.

Jany. 2nd, 1804

"I hope you have altered your mind about writing to Lowry. You know that he has often odd ideas, and I see no advantage to arise from one brother standing on ceremony with another. With respect to what you say concerning the friendship that existed between us, and the footing you were likely to be on with your family, I cannot well agree with you. It was always my wish to make friends of my brothers, particularly of you, which I must say has never entirely succeeded, from what cause I cannot say.

Altho' few families wish each other so well, yet there always has appeared to be some jealousies between us which has hitherto interrupted that particular degree of friendship I should wish for, but without success! Altho' this is my opinion on the subject, yet it may be far from the true cause....

For my part I am conscious I have often given my opinion to my brothers too freely perhaps, but as it has proceeded from an error of judgment and not from the heart, I hope for their pardon.

Your ever attached,
W. W. C."

In the course of these letters Dean Cole had commented on the number of losses that had marked the two years since his brother sailed for India. One more was to be soon added: in September 1804 at Florence Court, on a Sunday morning, the dean was found dead in his bed, having gone to it to all appearances in full health and vigour, only thirty years old.

Arthur Cole did not return to England till he had completed thirty years' service with distinction and rewards: as early as 1812, he spoke of retiring in six years with twenty-five to thirty thousand pounds. His relations with Lowry Cole were for long tinged with a sense that his elder brother was disposed to "consider him as a boy all his life"; and he complained that "there has been in our family a feeling of seniority which amounted almost to tyranny". It added to the estrangement of absence. But, when on his way home at last from India, he broke his journey at Mauritius for nearly a year to be Lowry Cole's guest, it was a real knitting of ties, to the delight of both.

CHAPTER III

MAIDA

THE Peace of Amiens made only a brief and delusive respite; war began again in 1803. In Ireland a shock to public tranquillity was given by Emmet's abortive insurrection in July of that year, which showed that the Irish Government had been taken by surprise, that the embers of revolt smouldered, and that they could easily be fanned into flame by help from France. But in 1804 Bonaparte had more formidable schemes than an Irish landing: he had begun to prepare the great flotilla which for long months threatened southern England across the narrow channel.

Lowry Cole was now by favour of the Duke of York commanding a company of the 3rd Dragoon Guards. But in August of that year he exchanged once more, and for the last time, into the regiment to which family associations specially bound him, the 27th Inniskilling Fusiliers.

The family correspondence of this period suggests the troubled times. In the summer of 1804, after her father's death, Lady Elizabeth Magenis, the least prosperously married of the sisters, wrote to her brother Arthur in India:

"You'll be surprised to hear I and my children are at Florence Court. Willy [the Dean of Waterford] and I have been keeping house here for these three months past. Magenis has gone . . . into the Fermanagh militia, of which he is Lieut.-Colonel. John [Lord Enniskillen] insisted on his going in. And being obliged (as every man is) in these perilous times to take an active part, he thought it best to join a corps like the Fermanagh, where besides the comfort of him and John being together he has the additional pleasure of thinking they would not desert him, for there never was a better set of men, and almost all of the right sort. . . . We have given up Chanter Hill, which Stewart has taken and where he now lives, and I am at present without any other home than this, which dearest John, with his usual kindness, insisted I should consider my own till times were a little settled. Our scheme of going to England was put a stop to by Bonaparte's threats which still hang over us! Lowry is at Chelmsford and very well and likes his situation, I believe, very much. He has Marlbank and intends building there, but *vile Boni* keeps us all in disagreeable situations—I have not seen my dearest Florence [Balfour] this year and a half—a long time."

Lowry Cole was at Chelmsford with his company of the Guards. Marlbank was a minor estate belonging to the family, with a house facing Lough Macnean on the borders of Fermanagh and Cavan. He had inherited this property on his father's death.

Meanwhile, the deaths of Lord and Lady Enniskillen within a few months of one another made the disposal of Henrietta Cole something of a problem to the brothers and sisters. She was a beautiful creature, tall, with auburn hair and a lovely complexion, very much admired in Dublin; but Dublin gaieties were despised by Irish people since the Union Society went to London to be amused. Her sisters' homes were in Ireland. Fortunately Lady Carhampton solved the difficulty by an invitation to stay with her in London. She wrote to her brother Lowry for his permission to accept. In this letter we realise the difficulties of travelling even within the British Isles in those troubled days.

"My dear Henrietta,   Chelmsford
                                                   Octr 25, 1804

I received your letter this morning. I can see no possible objection to your accepting Lady Carhampton's offer, particularly since both your sisters wish it. The only question therefore is how you are to go to town. I could with pleasure go for you were it in my power, but independent of not thinking it right to ask leave of absence at this time, it would be impossible to get it. You must therefore either come with Miss Wheeler, or go to Townley Hall [Lady F. Balfour's near Drogheda] where I can send my servant Pat (*alias* William in England) to meet you and escort you to London where we shall meet—if the French do not prevent us.

The latter is perhaps the best plan as the idea of an invasion is not yet over. If you prefer the former Wynne could perhaps send one of his servants part of the way and I could meet you on the road.

I own I am sorry Sally [Lady S. Wynne] goes to Ireland, as I have no doubt it is the principal object of the French, and we have had too melancholy a proof of late of the imbecility of the Irish government to trust much to them. However those who are there ought to know best. I have been here from the 14th of this month having exchanged into the 1st Battalion of the Regiment. Bess [Lady E. Magenis] I find remains at Florence Court, and Enniskillen has joined his regiment."

Lady Henrietta's stay in England as a young lady in the marriage market was not of very long duration, and the results were satisfactory to her brother. She seems to have kept house for him during part of the time. But in the summer of 1805 both Lowry Cole and Lady Henrietta were staying at Durnford in Wiltshire with the Hon. Mrs. Robinson, sister of Lady Malmesbury (whose sprightly correspondence with the young Lord Cole has been already given). With Mrs. Robinson was also Lady Malmesbury's daughter, the Hon. Frances Harris; and Lowry Cole, recovered from the wound dealt by "Kitty Pakenham", fell in love again. It seems that Lady Henrietta took the romance under her care out of a fellow-feeling; for she herself was on the verge of an engagement with Lord Grantham, who was a connection of Frances, being nephew of her aunt Mrs. Robinson. When exactly Lowry Cole's attachment came to be a tacit engagement we cannot say: but a letter from Frances Harris on June 28th, 1805, suggests that it was already of importance in her eyes to accept the affection offered her by Cole's sister.

"I needed no additional motive dear Lady Henrietta to bestow upon you *more* than a *small portion* of my affection; but I trust both yourself and Lord

Grantham will do me the justice to believe the connection you are about to form will not contribute to lessen either of you in my esteem.

"I accept with gratitude and pleasure the appellation of *sister* and feel sure a longer and more intimate acquaintance will confirm the predilection we felt for each other, and which though begun by chance seemed to prophecy we should some time or other be more nearly connected. Sincerely do I wish you my dear Lady Henrietta every happiness. . . ."

Lowry Cole was to furnish a pattern of constancy; there was no formal engagement and by the rules of that day he and his lady could not correspond; but this attachment lasted during ten years while he was abroad on active service, which began within a few months after that visit to Wiltshire and their first meeting.

The year 1805 found the nations of Europe trying to form such alliances with each other as would enable them to oppose Napoleon with success. Pitt spared neither effort nor money in making a coalition between England, Russia, Austria and Sweden, while Francis II, the new Emperor of Austria, signed a treaty with Prussia. But independence was given by Napoleon to the Rhine Provinces, Switzerland and Italy, Bavaria, Baden and Würtemberg. Crowned Emperor by the Pope and at the apex of his career, he had decided to deal his chief enemy, England, a death-blow; and a lofty scaffolding was prepared for him to mount and watch the success of his army crossing the Channel in their flat-bottomed boats. Years after, in 1815, when the fantastic attempt must have seemed almost legendary, this gaunt erection still remained at Boulogne to excite the curiosity of the passing traveller.

But by a sudden change of plan Napoleon marched his armies to the Danube; an Austrian army, under Mack, surrendered at Ulm on October 20th, and the Emperor crushed the Russians and Austrians at Austerlitz. He had himself crowned King of Italy at Milan, and his armies once again overran the Peninsula. Naples was forced to become his ally.

Such success must have seemed overwhelming. One after another he crushed his enemies—all but England, and once again she retaliated by means of her incomparable Nelson and the wooden walls of her ships. The following letter from Lord Malmesbury to his daughter Frances Harris shows the effect in England of the news of Trafalgar:

"To the Honble Frances Harris.

LONDON, *Wednesday*
Novr 6, 1805

MY DEAREST FANNY,
  Ring your bells, light your bonfires, fire your guns and illuminate all Cirencester!

The combined Fleet (France and Spain) is completely destroyed by Nelson off Cadiz! He himself fell in the midst of Triumph and Victory. An ending worthy of his glorious life. 19 ships of the line taken, one blown up.

Our Force 27, the French and Spaniards 33 ships.

The battle took place on the 21st Oct^r, lasted

four hours and terminated as I have just said—but I will enclose you the Bulletin from the Admiralty, which however will probably come out before the post in the shape of a Gazette Extraordinary.

Never was victory more glorious, more honourable, to the Victor or more opportune. It balances Mack's disgraceful surrender, and it is singular that on the day Buonaparte was declaiming that he wanted nothing but Colonies, Commerce and Ships, an event so very contradictory to his wants should have occurred.

Nelson, I hear, died almost instantly. A musket ball from the Tops wounded him on the shoulder and probably dropped through the cavity of the stomach on some vital part. Admiral Villeneuve is taken. *La Santissima Trinidad* of 130 guns sunk (after the action). In short it is (if possible) even greater than the victory of the Nile. And as that was a signal that roused the continent and produced Suvarrow's Campaign, I hail the omen!

I repeat it fully weighs down the wretched event at Ulm—with this difference to us—that it was the consequence of a severe well fought battle, with an enemy of superior force off his own coast. Buonaparte was in direct contrary predicament.

If we have no foolish continental peace but persevere *there* and well as *here*, I predict his extermination now as certain. In the mean time we must look for more disasters . . . but these must not dismay us, nor ought to dismay our allies. . . .

Read all my news to Lords Pembroke and Bathurst.

5 o'clock. Accounts just received that the Prussians have restored the Regency at Hannover and

that the whole Electorate except the fortress of Hamelin is now under its legitimate government. If, as it is expected, the Prussians besiege it, it will produce hostilities between them and the French. An event much to be wished.

This great naval victory and the news from Hannover will give the comfort and satisfaction to the King."

Lowry Cole in August was ordered to Malta, where he assumed command of the Inniskillings; and the correspondence helps us to carry on both the family and the public history. It will be noticed that on November 3rd, Cole at Malta had neither heard the news of Trafalgar nor of Austerlitz.

MALTA
"My dearest Henrietta, *Novr 3, 1805*
    I had just finished a letter full of bile to you for not writing to me—I had not had a line from you since I sailed from England—but on receiving your letter and his [her husband, Lord Grantham] I put my own with all my resentment in the fire.

Most cordially and from my heart do I congratulate you on the choice you have made, as from the little I know of him, I am sure he will make you happy, and with the most I know of you, I am equally sure you will make him so. I may now tell you which I did not do at the time, that my reason for wishing you to go to town was to give Grantham an opportunity of being better acquainted with you, as I thought he liked you. By the by you must look out for an housekeeper for me at Marlbanke as you have chosen to dispose of yourself elsewhere!

An expedition under the command of Sir James Craig sails tomorrow, in which I have got a very fine Brigade, so God be with you and every blessing is the sincere wish of
Your affec^{ate} Brother
G. L. Cole"

To Lord Grantham on his marriage.

MALTA
Novr 1805
"My dear Grantham,

I had suspected when in London that you liked Henrietta and most truly happy am I that my suspicions proved true, for I know no one I should have preferred to you. I have only one objection to you! Namely that you live at too great a distance from us all.

However it will be an inducement to me to live more in England than I otherwise intended to do. I hear your taste is much condemned by the Misses in taking a tall awkward Irish Miss! However I will say for her she has a most affectionate heart.

My first wish on leaving England was to hear of her being settled comfortably, and without flattery to you I could scarce hope she would be as fortunate as she has been.

If you will consider me as a brother (who already consider you as such in the true meaning of the word) and will write sometimes you will make me very happy. You will probably hear something of me before you receive this, as an expedition sails tomorrow under the command of Sir James Craig."

"To Lady Grantham. Torre dell'Annunziata
10 miles from Naples
9 Dec*r* 1805

I had written to you from Malta *via* Trieste, but I fear from the sad disasters of the Austrians that there is little chance of your receiving my letter.

I arrived here with the British army and landed on the 22nd of Nov*r* 8000 strong.

Sir James Craig Commander-in-Chief.
Sir John Stewart 2nd in command.
My friend Brodrick commands the reserve.
Brig^dier^ Genl Acland the 1st Brigade.
Brig^dier^ Genl Cole the 2nd Brigade.

The reserve have begun their march for the Frontier and I expect to follow in a day or two. We were joined at sea by 14000 Russians. General Lacy who commands them is an Irishman and is to have the Chief Command."

This was General Maurice de Lacey of Grodno, member of a Limerick family whose fighting men left Ireland with the Wild Geese under Sarsfield. One of them, Peter Count de Lacey, became a Field-Marshal in the Russian service, entering it when Peter the Great chose a hundred foreign officers to train his troops.

Maurice de Lacey, born in Limerick about 1740, no doubt got into the Russian Service by Peter's interest. He lived on till 1820 and is said by British officers who served with him to have had an incredible brogue, to have brought a nightcap to councils of war and put it on during discussion, but to have been simple, true-hearted and (in his own phrase) "always for fighting".

MAIDA

The expedition was bound for Southern Italy, where they were to co-operate with the Neapolitan army and the Russian corps referred to by Cole. But this small and miscellaneous force had scarcely crossed the Neapolitan frontier when the news of Austerlitz came to hand; telling also that Napoleon had placed his brother Joseph on the throne of Naples in place of the reigning Bourbons. The Bourbon King and Queen retired to Sicily, leaving their army to face the French. The Russians and the English also departed, the former to Corfu and the latter to Sicily, where the Fleet was at hand. The French army, commanded by Masséna, overran Italy.

Lowry Cole wrote to Lady Grantham from Messina, March 28th, 1806:

"If Grantham can find time from the bustle of the Metropolis—where I expect this will find you—I shall thank him to give me a little insight into the present state of politics, as Mr. Pitt's death seems to have made a strange change in affairs. I shall write to him by the next mail and let him know what is doing in this part of the world. No doubt you have been informed (long before this reaches you) of our allied army leaving the Kingdom of Naples, and our subsequent arrival here. The French are now in complete possession of the whole of Italy and are determined, it is said, to drive us out of the country. However, I hope and think they will find it a much more difficult thing to do than they pretend to say it is. The country is to all appearance in our favour, and would be very happy if we took possession of this island [Sicily] for ourselves. But that, I hope, we have too much honour to do, however advantageous it might be for England."

Meanwhile in Italy the Neapolitan *bourgeoisie* accepted the rule of King Joseph, but the peasants of the Apennines and of Calabria rose in rebellion and carried on a guerilla warfare.

The French army was a good deal scattered, and it was under a misconception of their numbers in Calabria that Sir John Stuart, now commanding the British, planned—with the consent of the Court at Palermo—a raid on General Regnier's forces at Maida.

The British troops, convoyed by Sir Sidney Smith's ships, left Messina on June 29th, 1806. They consisted of about 4600 men. The expeditionary force was wholly destitute of cavalry; sixteen Dragoon orderlies told off to the Brigadiers constituted its whole mounted force. There were ten mountain guns packed on mules and one field battery of six guns with about 150 artillerymen.

The expeditionary force landed in the Bay of Santa Eufemia on a shingly beach a mile below the high-lying village of the same name. The plain of Maida, intersected by the Lamato, a shallow river, is surrounded by wooded hills and occupies the narrowest part of the Peninsula. The villages of Santa Eufemia and Nicastro are on the north and Monteleone to the south of the plain.

While the British were occupied with landing and providing for a possible retreat, General Regnier made a forced march of seventy miles from Reggio in three days and took up his position on the wooded heights at the east of the plain in the village of San Pietro di Maida.

Major Roverea, General Cole's A.D.C., tells the story of the battle:

"The 4th July at 4 o'clock in the morning we moved forward in four columns—Colonel Kempt covering the left, General Acland and General Cole across a marshy plain, Colonel Oswald along the seashore. Sir Sidney was anchored three or four miles from the land. Four companies of the Watteville [Swiss] regiment were left at the Tower of Santa Eufemia. At 7 o'clock we halted and assembled the army near the shore. General Stuart and his Staff went to reconnoitre the enemy and I followed with General Cole. The French occupied a very strong position on a wooded hill at the other side of the plain. In order to attack them we should have had a long march and to cross the Lamato and finally to climb the hill covered with scattered trees and bushes which could be defended foot by foot and would cost us many lives. Imagine our surprise and joy when we saw the French troops leave this advantageous position and descend into the plain! Our advance guard and General Acland had orders to advance. It was eight o'clock.

"A short time after General Cole and Colonel Oswald also advanced first in line and then in column. I was sent to throw some 'Flankers' in the reeds on our right beyond the Lamato. When I returned our line was formed—the Light Brigade on the right, then from right to left, General Acland, Colonel Oswald and General

Cole.[1] Our guns and those of the enemy began the engagement.

"The *coup d'œil* was magnificent—our fine troops as steady and in as good order as on the parade ground, *vis-à-vis* the French also in line, their arms glittering in the sun. I had never seen anything of the sort before and the sight struck me with admiration.

"At 9 o'clock all the enemy's line advanced on us and the battle began. For a quarter of an hour the firing was very hot. Our people, aiming well, threw the ranks of the enemy into confusion. After that, our Battalion of Light Infantry made a charge with the bayonet and cut their Light Infantry Brigade almost to pieces. General Acland's Brigade followed up the charge and on our right the enemy, completely routed, was flying in all directions, letting themselves be killed or taken prisoners, for they could not run as fast as our men who had thrown away their accoutrements. On the left, on our side the combat did not go so well for us, for some sharp-shooters had come close enough to incommode us with their fire.

"While my General was thinking that he ought not to allow some 'Flankers' to dislodge them, a shell exploded quite close to us and set fire to the dried grass of the field in which we were, and very soon the whole was in flames, and this accident caused some confusion in the centre of the 27th

---

[1] Kempt had the Light Brigade composed of the Light companies of the 8 battalions: Acland the 2nd Bn. 78th, 1st Bn. 58th, and 1st Bn. 81st Regiments: Oswald's Brigade was formed of de Watteville's Swiss: Cole had the 1st Bn. 27th (Inniskillings) and a battalion composed of the light grenadier companies.
The 20th Regiment was sent to act independently along the coast.

MAIDA

Regiment. But the smoke prevented the enemy from perceiving this. At the same time a body of their Cavalry advanced and threatened our left flank and appeared to be about to charge. So much so that our mounted officers drew sword or pistol and prepared to defend themselves in the mêlée. Two companies of Grenadiers who were moved from the right of the Brigade to reinforce the left, suffered very much. A mass of infantry advanced behind the enemy Cavalry and the moment became critical for us. General Cole threw back 3 Companies of the 27th with 2 of the Grenadiers, and still the enemy advanced.

"At this instant the 20th arrived, their advance through the bushes having concealed them from the French, joined our left wing, and took up their position behind the left of our Brigade. This unexpected reinforcement disconcerted the enemy."

Rapidly forming up on Cole's left rear, the 20th brushed aside the French sharp-shooters, repulsed their cavalry with one deadly volley and then, changing front to right, so completely enfiladed the enemy's line that Regnier immediately ordered a retreat. The French army was in flight. No pursuit was possible, there being no cavalry, and Sir John Stuart thought the success achieved was sufficient, for he withdrew his troops and embarked them for Sicily.

Sir Charles Oman says of this battle:

"It had no political or military results. It had as its sole good result the confirming in the minds of the more intelligent British officers who had taken part in it of the great truth of the superiority of Line tactics over Column tactics. It was of no small importance that a very appreciable number of the men who were to take an honourable part in the Peninsular War had their first experience of fighting on a considerable scale on the Calabrian shore....

"The whole fate of the battle of Maida turned on the first clash of arms between Kempt (the Light Brigade) and the 1st Légère. It was the fairest fight between Column and Line that had been seen since the Napoleonic wars began. On the French side two heavy columns of 800 men each, drawn up in columns of companies, *i.e.* with a front of some 60 men each and a depth of 14. The front of each was not more than 60 yards. Kempt, on the other hand, had his battalion in line two men deep only, so that, even deducting officers, sergeants, etc., he had a front of 350 yards, only 120 yards of which had Frenchmen directly in front of it."

Other authorities consider that the moral effect of this victory was very great, as it proved that Napoleon's veterans were not invincible.

General Cole and Colonel Haviland Smith (in command of the Inniskillings) received gold medals —of which only seventeen were issued. The Inniskilling Fusiliers (27th) received the thanks of Parliament and the royal authority to bear the word "Maida" on its colours, and at long last, in 1847, a clasp inscribed "Maida" was awarded to all surviving officers and men.

Again to quote Oman:

"But for all those who were present or who

received the report of an intelligent eye-witness the little-remembered Calabrian battle of Maida was an epoch-making day in British military history.

"On the sandy plain of the Lamato 5000 Infantry in line received the shock of 6000 in column and inflicted on them one of the most crushing defeats on a small scale that took place during the whole war, disabling or taking prisoners 2000 men with a total loss to themselves of only 320. The troops and the order of the battle won the victory, for the commander, Stuart, was an incapable officer whose personality had no influence on the fight and who sacrificed all the fruits of his success by his torpidity.

"But the moral was unmistakable. On the critical point of the field four battalions of the best troops of the old French army in Italy, in Columns of Division, had been met in frontal shock and blown to pieces by three British battalions in two-deep line. The losses had been fearful of the vanquished, those of the victors trifling.

"As I have observed elsewhere, some of the officers who were afterwards to be Wellington's most trusted lieutenants were present at Maida and understood its meaning, among them Cole, who later commanded the 4th Division in the Peninsula, Brigadier Kempt, Oswald and Colborne."

Cole's own account is given in a letter to Lady Grantham:

MONTELEONE
"MY DEAREST HENRIETTA,   11*th July*, 1806

As you will probably have heard before this reaches you of our arrival in this country and the consequent defeat of the French army on the 4th inst., I flatter myself you will not be sorry to hear I am well and have escaped untouched.

I must refer you to the Gazette for the details and have only to say that, if I may be allowed to judge, the action is not less honourable to our arms than those that took place in the Egyptian expedition last war. Our loss has been trifling, that of the enemy considerable. Everything is due to the steadiness and good discipline and gallantry of the troops, without which we must have been defeated as they were near twice our number—with cavalry also, of which we had none.

We are now on our way back to Sicily as we have not a force sufficient to defend the country against what may and probably will be sent against us. The last account we had of the French they were retiring in great confusion to Cortona. General Reynier, the Commander-in-Chief, is said to be wounded."

The British Expeditionary Force had a very dull, unsatisfactory sojourn in Sicily. It suffered a good deal from malaria. It was supposed that when Murat assumed command of 50,000 troops he would drive the British out of Sicily. He did indeed surprise and capture the island of Capri, our advanced post in the Bay of Naples, but, satisfied with this success, he did not attack our main position on the Strait of Messina. On the part of the British a few rather unsuccessful raids, a brilliant episode in the defence and subsequent evacuation of the Castle of Scilla seem to have failed to interest, at any rate, General Cole. In the few letters of this date he says how tired he is of doing nothing, with no prospect of active service although he had been promoted Major-General in April 1808; and the earnest wish he expresses is to leave Sicily and if possible get out to Spain, which was beginning to be the centre of military interest, as Napoleon himself was taking command there. Failing a post in Spain, Cole longed to return to England and his beloved family. He wrote to Lady Grantham:

MESSINA

"MY DEAREST HENRIETTA,   *7th Nov.*, 1808

. . . Believe me, I am equally as anxious to see you all as you can be to see me, and should ere this have asked permission to return to England but for the critical situation this island has been supposed to be in since Sir John Moore left us. The taking of Capri by the French and the arrival of their new King Joachim [Murat] at Naples (who is a military character) has strengthened that opinion. I therefore could not, nor cannot think of leaving it as long as this continues without I am recalled, which I had hoped would have been the case, on my promotion, and which, notwithstanding the above supposition, had it been so I should have taken advantage of it. If nothing happens before the Spring I shall endeavour to see you, if only for a short time.

I have lately been making a tour of the island, which I never had an opportunity of doing before since my arrival here. . . .

Your account of Charlotte [Lady Enniskillen] vexes me, but I trust your apprehensions are groundless and that the next Packet will bring me the account of an increase of the Cole name having taken place. I am the more anxious about it as I begin to think that his Lordship's is the only branch of the family likely to increase as God knows when this war will end and until it does I have no idea of matrimony. Time will tell, and such resolutions are often broken!"

The next letter announces his appointment to Sir Arthur Wellesley's Staff in Spain. But before entering on the new chapter of Lowry Cole's very successful career in the Peninsula, one may collect from the family correspondence glimpses of another part of England's effort in these momentous years.

On January 8th, 1806, while Joseph Bonaparte was entering Naples, and Lowry Cole was with the British Expeditionary Force in Sicily, Arthur Cole wrote to his sister Lady Grantham from India.

> Head Quarters Grand Army
> Camp at SAGUSWAND GHAUT
> On the left bank of the Hyphasis river

"MY DEAR HENRIETTA,
You must, my dear sister, excuse my very long silence. So many misfortunes have occurred to us since my last letter that I have not had courage to write to you or to anyone of my family except, I believe, once to Florence [Lady F. Balfour]. I have never heard from you, but have been told that one of your letters was in the Packet of the last captured Indiaman. I therefore thank you for it, altho' I did not enjoy the gratification of receiving it.

I trust, my Love, that your health and spirits are recovered after the death of our adored William: from your being at Florence Court when that fatal blow was inflicted, they both must have suffered a cruel shock. . . .

I left Calcutta last April to accompany Col. Malcolm on an Embassy to one of the Mahratta Courts.

We joined the Grand Army near Agra under Gen. Lake in May, and have remained with it ever since. In the month of November his Lordship again took the field after Rao Holkar. We pursued the army of that chief into this country [the Punjab], where our enemy having requested terms Peace was granted him.

We are now about to march back to Delhi, from which place the army will be dispersed into cantonments and Col. Malcolm and I shall return to Calcutta.

The last six months have been the pleasantest I have passed since my arrival in this country, the scene being more active than heretofore, and as it was a military one more congenial to my wishes. Colonel Malcolm and I live in the family of Lord Lake, which is large and composed of many fine young men.

You will perhaps accuse me of want of gallantry from my having told you I preferred the last six months of my residence in India (in which period I have scarcely seen a lady) to any other time I have passed in this detested country, but you will be wrong, Netty, for I assure you no man admires your sex more than I do when you are amiable, and none can enjoy the society of ladies to a greater degree. . . .

We are not, however, blessed with many Indian Ladies, which is perhaps fortunate for me who am a most determined Bachelor."

CHAPTER IV

FIRST EXPERIENCES IN THE PENINSULA

Lowry Cole's last letter was from Sicily in November 1808, and when he returned to England does not appear. But in order to understand the frame of mind in which he received, in September 1809, his definite orders to join Wellington's army, it is necessary to recall briefly the events in the Peninsula during the interval.

Sir John Moore's advance into Spain and subsequent retreat, terminating in January 1809 with the battle of Corunna and the re-embarkation of the British Expeditionary Force, seemed to have marked the end of one of Castlereagh's efforts against Napoleon. The ten thousand British in Portugal commanded by Cradock from Lisbon, even though supplemented by some raw Portuguese levies under British officers, were hopelessly insufficient to oppose the French armies. There were three immediately available to invade Portugal and Andalusia; Soult's army in the north, Lapisse's about Salamanca in the north-east and Victor's in the Tagus Valley east of Lisbon. Napoleon, who was himself shortly to leave the Peninsula, issued orders for these armies to make a combined advance on Portugal co-operating with each other. Soult's objective was Lisbon, with Lapisse to protect his left flank, and Victor was directed on Cadiz. But the French had difficulties of supply and

FIRST EXPERIENCES IN THE PENINSULA

unfavourable conditions of weather and natural features to overcome which rendered their advance slow and ill-harmonised. Soult displayed the most energy and, leaving a detachment to control Galicia for which he was responsible, advanced and took Oporto on March 29th, 1809. His further advance southwards was delayed by swollen rivers, Spanish risings in his rear, and fears of risk on his left owing to Lapisse's immobility.

Meanwhile Cradock's force, which in face of the threatening storm had been prepared for re-embarkation, was reinforced. The British Government, encouraged by French hesitation, had changed its mind. In addition to reinforcement Beresford was sent to reorganise the Portuguese, helped by a number of British officers. More important, Wellesley, who since October 1808 had been in England, was sent back to Portugal, this time in undisputed supreme command; and he arrived on April 22nd, 1809, just about the time Napoleon was leaving Spain and handing over control to Joseph: a control which most of the French generals resented.

Wellesley was not slow in justifying his Government's decision. Advancing north, he made his famous crossing of the Douro and recaptured Oporto on May 12th, 1909. He then, in cooperation with the Spaniards, turned on Victor's army, and the latter, reinforced by Joseph, sought a decision, attacking Wellesley on ground of his selection at Talavera. The British losses were heavy but the victory complete. These successes earned Wellesley his first step in the peerage and as will be seen, it was Lord Wellington's army that Cole was ordered to join.

But Cole's letter shows that the recent victories had not effaced the impression that the Peninsula adventure was still a risky one. The miserable failure of the Walcheren expedition seemed a warning and Cole had not yet realised the difference that Wellington's leadership would make. After receiving orders to proceed from Sicily to England, and thence to Portugal, he wrote to his brother-in-law, as he passed through London.

31 Duke St., W.
5*th Sept.*, 1809

"My dear Grantham,

I would have written to you or Henrietta sooner to have informed you of my appointment to the Staff of Lord Wellington's army and the impossibility of my being able to see you at Newby as I had proposed, but I had supposed Robinson had done so, as it was by a letter from him desiring my immediate return in consequence of the Horse Guards' intentions. I, of course, lost no time and arrived here last Friday in the mail and I expect to be off to Lisbon in the course of this week or the next. . . .

In the opinion of most people my stay will not be long, as it is supposed Lord Wellington cannot resist the force against him. I cannot find out whether it is the intention of government to send more troops there or not, but hope some of those returning from Flushing will go.

By the bye, that, as I feared, turned out a bad business and may shake the present ministry, but I hope it will not, although they deserve it for sending Lord Chatham to command. It was evident that it could only have been done by marching directly

FIRST EXPERIENCES IN THE PENINSULA

upon Antwerp and not proceeding as they did in the old jog-trot way of taking every little fort previously. Lord Chatham ought to have known that the more time he gave the French to collect troops, the more difficulty he would find."

On his arrival in Portugal Cole found that the active operations of 1809 were over. Wellington had initiated the preparation of the lines of Torres Vedras, realising that the French would not accept defeat but would return in greater force. Meanwhile, in the winter 1809-10, the allied forces were distributed in groups covering the frontier and waiting till the French intentions could be learnt. It was a period of reorganisation, especially of the Portuguese troops, since the failure of the Spaniards showed Wellington that he would chiefly have to rely on these for assistance. The French had 360,000 men in Spain and though many of these were dispersed controlling the Spanish guerillas in the various provinces, yet the numbers were sufficient to furnish formidable armies for the invasion of Portugal. During this pause Cole's post was at Guarda behind the frontier fortress of Almeida on the high ground between the Tagus and Douro valleys.

There he assumed command of the 4th Division, which included the Inniskillings who had fought under him at Maida. Some idea of the personality of the man under whom the Division was to become famous should now be given, as it was appraised by one who knew him well.

Major Roverea, his A.D.C., whose description of the battle of Maida has been already quoted, was Swiss and probably belonged to de Watteville's regiment in the first instance. Louis de Watteville, its war-tried Colonel, and most of the officers, were Swiss patriots who had quitted their native land after its wanton conquest by the French in 1798, and the core of the rank and file were old Swiss soldiers of a similar type.

In his letters Major Roverea gives an account of his first meeting with General Cole at Valetta in Malta in 1805:

"I had dined with General Brodrick. . . . The next day he surprised me by coming to see me. He introduced me to Brigadier-General Cole, who had also dined with him. General Cole is a young man 32 years of age, with very polished manners and great charm, and belonging to one of the first families in Ireland. He told me that both General Villette and General Brodrick having strongly recommended me to him, he wished to appoint me his Brigade Major. I accepted his offer with empressement, and on the 15th was put on his Staff. A short time after Sir James Craig offered to put me on his own Staff, but I preferred being General Cole's Brigade Major because I looked upon him as a friend and a father. I knew that, however great the advantages of being with the Commander-in-Chief might be, they would not compensate me for the delightful society which I enjoyed with General Cole, who seems to have it at heart to form and instruct me. Already he shows me more confidence than I have any right to expect. He heaps kindness on me and gives me a thousand proofs of his attachment. To give you an idea of this, he often says, as you used to do, 'Hold yourself up', or when he

FIRST EXPERIENCES IN THE PENINSULA

laughs at my horsemanship or my awkwardness about carving at table. He has taught me a number of little secrets, trifles that one must be careful to observe, which one would not think of perhaps, but which are sufficiently important to make one appear *comme il faut* or the contrary if one neglects them. Some of these habits are of universal application, others more concern English ideas.

"General Cole is very warm-hearted and sincere. He is very much attached to his family and is adored by them. He is a keen soldier and would go to the end of the world in pursuit of his profession. He is also an excellent mechanic, has very good taste and understands better than anyone how to keep a comfortable ménage."

Cole was noted for the excellence of the dinners which he gave in winter quarters during the Peninsular War. Wellington is said to have remarked: "Cole gives the best dinners, Hill the next best, mine are no great things, and Beresford's and Picton's are very bad indeed".

Probably there is no human link stronger than that between a Commanding Officer and his Staff. They live in close intimacy, share the same dangers and the same hardships, learn to appreciate each other's merits and to make allowance for each other's shortcomings. General Cole was evidently very fond of Roverea and appreciated his faithful affection. Indeed, he and his Staff were a very happy family, to judge from letters. Roverea was with him from 1805 to 1813, when he was killed at the battle of Sauroren, greatly to his beloved General's sorrow.

Cole's letters from Guarda are chiefly of interest for the growing confidence that they show in his chief.

"To Lady Grantham.
Private to all but Grantham and Robinson.

28th February, 1810
GUARDA

MY DEAREST HENRIETTA,
... It is true I have not written often, but then I have had more to do than I ever had before, and I am one of those who do not think it right for a military man to commit his opinions on men and measures of an army to paper. I have really nothing else except respecting my own faulty self to write about. ...

If a mere military life among strangers, at least who were perfectly so to me when I joined, could make me happy, I am so. I never served under any chief I liked so much—Sir John Moore excepted—as Lord Wellington. He has treated me with much more confidence than I had a right or could have expected from anyone. Few, I believe, possess a firmer mind or have, so far as I have heard, more the confidence of the army. Whatever may be the result, I think and hope it will be honourable to us if not successful. I have to regret on his own account as well as that of the public that he ever gave his mind to anything but his profession, as his entering into politics has created (as it always does in England) many political enemies which prevent him receiving that credit his abilities and services have entitled him to.

I arrived here on the 11th last month after a

FIRST EXPERIENCES IN THE PENINSULA

march of about 300 miles. It is the highest habitable place in Portugal and one of the highest, I believe, in Europe. The thermometer was for some days as low as 29. I live in the Palace belonging to the Bishop. It was built and, I believe, never repaired since then—the year 1665, with furniture of the same date, I suppose, from its appearance; without a fireplace, long galleries and nothing but a pan of wood ashes to warm the room. Notwithstanding these numerous discomforts, I have enjoyed good health and have lived as I always endeavour to do. . . .

11th April, 1810.—It is just three months this day since I arrived in this mountain, and apparently there is less prospect of our having anything to do than when I arrived, except that the season is advancing. The enemy do not show any wish to attack us, and Lord Wellington is too hampered by affairs in England to venture another trip into Spain. You appear in England to be much more alarmed for us than we are for ourselves.

My present residence is called the Siberia of the army and if applied to the weather it certainly deserves the appellation, which, with a few exceptions of fair days, has scarce ceased raining or snowing—usually the latter.

Pray make Grantham write to me respecting the politics of the day and the probable duration of the present ministry, whom I think are determined to keep their places until (as a friend of mine says) they are pulled out of them. I am not an admirer of 'The Talents', but anything is better than a weak ministry in times like these. Pray how does Lord Cas. [Castlereagh] bear being out of office?"

The first main operation undertaken by the French in 1810 began in January when Soult, now appointed Joseph's Chief of Staff, overran Andalusia.
At the same time, however, forces were collected for the invasion of Portugal and the task of conquering the country and of driving the British into the sea was given to Masséna. His army numbered some 80,000, and this, advancing south-west from Salamanca, constituted Wellington's chief danger. Soult, however, was to co-operate by invading southern Portugal by way of Badajoz, and a detachment of Masséna's army required watching in the Tagus valley.
It was not till June that Masséna began to move, but, till by capture of the fortresses of Ciudad Rodrigo in July and of Almeida in the end of August, he had cleared his way, Wellington was not forced to retire before the advance. By the beginning of September the British retreat had commenced according to a well-thought-out plan which had as its key the lines of Torres Vedras.
Threatened by Masséna's main army and by the advance of Regnier's detachment down the Tagus valley, Wellington had issued orders to the Portuguese inhabitants to retire before the French advance and to take refuge behind the Torres Vedras lines. They were to lay waste their fields, break bridges and mills and leave nothing for the subsistence of the invaders. Wellington's army aimed only at giving time for this destruction to be

FIRST EXPERIENCES IN THE PENINSULA

thorough by fighting delaying actions. With this object at the end of September the Battle of Busaco was fought, in which Cole's Division played only a minor part. On the whole the retreat was carried out as planned, though neither the delaying action nor the destruction was as thorough as Wellington had hoped. Busaco brought Masséna to a halt, but owing to a misunderstanding on the part of a subordinate commander, Wellington's flank was exposed and Masséna was free to manœuvre him from the strong position, without, however, endangering his further retreat to Torres Vedras where the lines were securely occupied.

Masséna made no attempt to attack the lines but called for reinforcement. Wellington had hoped by laying waste the country to make it impossible for Masséna to maintain his position; but the process had not been sufficiently thorough, and in the Santarem neighbourhood sufficient was left to feed the French army till the beginning of March 1811.

By that time assistance which Masséna had hoped to receive from Soult was not forthcoming. The latter had indeed started and had captured Badajoz from the Spaniards but then had to retrace his steps to assist the force he had left investing Cadiz.

On March 5th Masséna had no alternative but to retreat; his army was already suffering from privations and they were to suffer more on their way back.

Before describing Cole's part in the battles of 1811 space may be found here for some letters which refer to incidents on the retreat from Guarda and during the occupation of Torres Vedras which throw light on the reputation Cole enjoyed, and give the atmosphere of the British Army of those times—not widely different from that of to-day.

One is written to his son by the son of General Sir George Napier, brother to the more famous conqueror of Scinde and to the historian of the Peninsular War:

11*th January*, 1882
OAKLANDS, COSHAM

"MY DEAR COLE,

In an MS. narrative by my father of his military life written in 1828 for his children, which has lately come into my possession, I find a passage relating to your father which I think will interest you. It was just after the battle of Busaco (where my father was wounded) while on the march to the lines of Torres Vedras, as follows:

'About the third day's march I was so ill and stiff with my wound that I could no longer sit my horse and was forced to get into a cart and make the best of my way to Lisbon. In the progress of which, one cold dark rainy night the Portuguese driver decamped and left his cart and myself sticking in the mud. Seeing a light at some distance, I got out of the cart and made my way to it, but was so exhausted with the pain and illness, having also the ague, that I sank down perfectly done up at the door of the house where the light proceeded, and luckily for me this was the quarters of my friend, Sir Lowry Cole, commanding the 4th Division, who, being informed that a wounded officer was at his door, immediately came down, had me carried in, gave me his own bed, had a surgeon sent for to dress my wound (the same who afterwards cut off my arm) and sent me a good dinner. After which

FIRST EXPERIENCES IN THE PENINSULA

I fell asleep and awoke next morning at daybreak, quite refreshed and able to get on with General Cole's Staff to the lines, where I took leave of my kind friend, the General, whose kindness to me I can never forget or cease to be grateful for as long as I live. But I am not a solitary instance of Sir Lowry Cole's kindness and generosity, for he never would permit officer or *private soldier* to want anything he had or that it was in his power to procure for them. And though a hot-tempered and passionate man, he is as kind and generous as he is brave, and a more truly gallant and enterprising soldier never breathed.'"

There is a delightful story about the retreat from Guarda to the lines of Torres Vedras, preserved in a letter from the General's soldier servant:

"The rear guard came in and passed the door of the house we were in, both horse and foot and artillery. It was here we lost poor little Dash. He never would quit the General, but when all was confusion he lost the General and went back to the house we had left, which was occupied that same night by the French General, who, seeing General Cole's name on his collar—'G. L. Cole, Major-General'—took care of Dash.

"The next day the retreat began on our old route through Thomar and Leiria until we came to the lines before Lisbon, which extended from Villa Franca on the Tagus to Torres Vedras on the seacoast, keeping Lisbon in an angle. Those lines were made before the retreat commenced and plenty of guns on them. The Tagus at Lisbon was crowded with men of war and the launches with a heavy gun in each sailing up and down.

"Here we remained for several weeks, the French looking at us and we looking at them. The French were getting short of provisions, while we were well supplied from the shipping, and the General had a fresh supply of wine and hams. All the supplies that the French could get were generally cut off by the Portuguese militia and the Spanish guerilla. There was a bullock going to be killed in the French lines that broke away from them and ran over to our lines. It was soon shot and skinned. The two hind-quarters were sent to the General and he sent one of them to Sir Thomas Picton of the 5th Division.

"That evening we herd [sic] a bugle sounding from the French. It was an officer, two sergeants and a bugler with a flag of truce. I don't know the cause of the flag of truce, but our General received a polite letter addressed to Major-General Cole for an exchange of prisoners and our joy was great when we saw our long-lost Dash led by one of the sergeants. When Dash was brought to the Quinta and heard the General's voice, one would think he was mad, and as soon as the door was opened he jumped on to the General's knee.

"The General ordered Captain Roverea to write a note to the French General to inform him that the bullock had been killed and divided, but he sent him his share. Many's the laugh there has been about poor Dash being a French prisoner!"

The same correspondent goes on to describe some diversions of the British army.

FIRST EXPERIENCES IN THE PENINSULA

"Some weeks after this the Division was ordered to Azembiza, another town on the Tagus, and here our whole family and staff met and were entertained at the General's cost. There was Captain Wade, Captain Roverea, A.D.C., Major Brooks acting A.M.G., Captain Barclay, A.G., Captain Magenis and his brother, a midshipman that came on leave to see his brother, besides servants, grooms, etc.

"Azembiza is a town on the Tagus. The boats from Lisbon came up loaded with everything necessary to supply us. . . . Everything respecting the family affairs went on well and we had horse-racing and such sporting gentlemen as Captain Mellish, Captain de Courcy, Captain Magenis and, last but not least, Captain Wade. They used to have donkey races and this was the best sport. The General gave a grand ball and many ladies, the wives and daughters of officers then in Lisbon, were invited. They all could come up in boats, mostly men-of-war boats. The Captain of the ship, Mr. Magenis, belonged and some of his fellow-officers."

CHAPTER V

ALBUERA

WHEN Masséna's retreat began he was pursued and harried to his great discomfiture; but Cole spent a few days only with the pursuing army, as his Division was detached by Wellington to reinforce Beresford. He joined the Marshal at a critical moment, as Beresford was commencing operations for the recapture of Badajoz.

A letter from Cole to Lady Grantham gives an account of his movements from leaving the lines of Torres Vedras onwards:

"Since Masséna commenced his retreat from Santarem, my Division has scarcely ceased marching—we have not marched less than 400 miles. We accompanied Lord Wellington as far as Condeixa. We turned off by Esperial back to Thomar and across the Tagus where we joined the second Division of the army under Marshal Beresford, forming a corps of 20,000 Effectives, the original destination of which was to raise the siege of Badajos, for which we were too late. We have retaken Campo Mayor and Olivença and I expect we shall invest Badajos in a few days, which I hope will not give us great trouble, having a weak garrison, except which there is not a French soldier in Estremadura, the whole of their force having abandoned the country at our approach and taken the road to Cordova.

ALBUERA

"I hope John Bull will be satisfied with Lord Wellington, who is certainly deserving of anything that can be said of him. Having driven Masséna out of Portugal, he is come to take the command of this army, which I hope, and it is not impossible, may take the direction of Seville, where the enemy are scarce strong enough to maintain themselves much longer even against the Spaniards without considerable reinforcements. This is merely conjecture on my part."

Marshal Beresford is prominent throughout the Peninsular War. When the Portuguese offered the command of all their troops to an English officer, Beresford was chosen for the post—Wellington having declined the appointment.

Beresford had seen much service previously, but through no fault of his own had missed success. He was gazetted a Portuguese marshal and started his task of training and disciplining the Portuguese army, a task for which he was well qualified. The results of his training soon began to show. But, excellent in ruling and training the troublesome Portuguese and producing discipline and order where there had been none, in the field Marshal Beresford was not a success. He lacked the power of quick decision, hesitated and lost his head; consequently his victories were won at great expense of life; so much so that after the bloody battle of Albuera, Wellington, writing privately to a friend, said: "Such another battle would ruin us; I am labouring hard to set all right again".

General Cole did not think highly of Beresford's talents as a soldier nor did he like him personally.

This opinion must have been confirmed by Beresford's mismanagement of the siege of Badajos, when he refused to listen to the advice of the engineers to make an attack simultaneously on the Castle and the Fort of San Christoval and contented himself with besieging the latter, saying that he would take that first. The consequence was that this small attack, comprising only six or eight guns and three regiments, 26th, 40th and 97th, had to support for three days with heavy loss the whole fire and efforts of the place and fort, being within a thousand yards of the former and four hundred and fifty from the latter.

On May 12th, 1811, Beresford, on hearing of the approach of Soult from the south of Spain, was obliged to raise the siege and collect his army and lead it to Albuera. General Cole's Division was employed in covering the removal of stores and only arrived on the field of Albuera when the battle had begun.

The scene of combat was a ridge four miles in length traversing the road from Seville and commanding that of Valverde in the rear, which would be the line of retreat in case of misfortune. The Albuera river crossed by a bridge ran in front, the ravine of a hill torrent behind.—I shall now quote from Major Roverea's journal:

"On the evening of the 15th May we received the order to raise the blockade and to join the army at Albuhera. I was on horseback all night and at two o'clock in the morning the advanced posts were withdrawn, the columns set in motion. General Cole had with him two Brigades of his Division[1]

[1] According to Napier, one of these brigades was Portuguese.

ALBUERA

and 3,000 Spaniards without coats and badly armed. During the same night General Beresford's corps had been joined at the camp of Albuhera by 4,000 men under General Ballesteros and by the troops brought by General Blake from Cadiz, 8,000 very fine troops.

"We arrived at Albuhera at 8 o'clock in the morning. Our force consisted of 30,000 men, of which 15,000 were Spanish, 7,000 English and 8,000 Portuguese. We only had 1,500 horses. A small stream, the Albuhera, flows through the village of the same name, crossed by a stone bridge. On the right of the brook there is an immense plain covered with forests. On the left bank the ground is more varied, being a chain of little hills uncultivated and treeless, covered with fern. Our Marshal did not believe that Soult would attack him, but that if he did, the bridge which was our centre would be his objective. The Spaniards were placed on the right as being the point least threatened, the English at the centre, the Portuguese on the left, forming a line parallel with the stream. General Cole with the 4th Division was in reserve at a certain distance on the right of the Spaniards. Five hundred paces from the right of the Spanish line was a hill which dominated our position, the possession of which was essential to our safety, which should have been fortified or at any rate held very strongly. The Marshal thought it sufficient to occupy it with 500 Spanish light troops. Under cover of a false attack on the bridge, screened by their numerous cavalry, the French occupied the fatal hill in force. Five minutes later we could see all the French infantry formed in close columns with 40 pieces of cannon commanding and enfilading our line."

From this moment the aim of Marshal Beresford was to dislodge the French from the hill. An English Brigade of the 2nd Division commanded by Colonel Colborne was brought from the centre and advanced alone to attack the French army, mounted the hill and were cut to pieces, losing 5 colours, 3 guns and 800 prisoners.

"Our Marshal bravely exposed himself, but gave no orders, and the officers on his Staff acted as they thought best. The rest of the second Division was brought up and deployed behind the Spaniards. Our people, never having seen the latter, mistook them for the enemy, and, while the Polish Lancers[1] charged the Spaniards in front, opened fire on them. I think that in the confusion the Spaniards did not realise this before means were taken to make them cease fire.

"The 2nd Division advanced in line, retrieved the Spanish force and, continuing for a few steps, placed themselves on the crest of the hill, and opened such a well-directed fire which, added to their great courage, makes the British infantry so superior to all other on the day of battle.

"At the first sound of the guns I was sent to the Marshal to accompany him and to receive his orders for my General. I received none. . . . General Cole, receiving no orders and observing that he was menaced by the enemy cavalry, had deployed his troops in line and formed a sharp

[1] In the French Service.

angle with the right of the Spanish line. . . . When General Cole saw that the 4th Division had replaced the Spaniards, he decided to attack the hill occupied by the enemy, on the possession of which evidently the fate of the battle depended. In undertaking this attack without having received an order from the Marshal, and in taking on himself the responsibility of a decisive movement, he acted with a moral courage of which few English generals have given an example.

"He placed a Portuguese Battalion in a square on the left of his Brigade of Fusiliers. The rest of the Portuguese Brigade advanced *'en potence'* and strengthened the attack of the British. Four picked English Companies formed in square on the right of the Portuguese to cover their flanks against the enemy's Cavalry.

"All this happened just at the moment when the Marshal, frightened by his losses and with no further hope of victory, had begun to evacuate the village of Albuhera and to give the first orders for the retreat. This retreat, with an enemy fortress (Badajos) and a river (Guardiana) without a bridge in our rear, and considering the superiority of their Cavalry, would have been very difficult to carry out.

"When the Marshal saw the 4th Division marching forward and when he regained some hope of success, he gave me the first and only order I received from him, which was to go to the rear and find a Spanish regiment which hadn't suffered much and take it to support the 4th Division. I executed the order. It was a Division of Guards Wallones. When I had directed the officer in command and shown him what he was to do, I left him and joined the Fusilier Brigade.

"My General and all his Staff were wounded, besides almost all the commanding officers. But in spite of a terrible fire of mitraille the Line advanced in good order and firing.

"We had retaken the lost guns and I was just pointing out to the General a Squadron of the enemy who were about to charge his Grenadiers when I was hit and fell from my horse. It was almost the end of the affair. The 2nd Division had advanced to support the 4th. It was the courage of the soldiers and the superiority of man to man which gained us the victory after a bloody combat. If the French when they had stretched out two-thirds of our men had marched forward and forced our line, we should have been lost. It is in such cases that individual courage counts. The French officers made every effort to keep their men, but the first ranks of their column threw themselves on those behind. They cried out that it was butchery and were soon in full flight. . . . Their superiority in Cavalry, our immense loss, the irresolution of the Marshal, who should have advanced the Portuguese, were the reasons we were unable to pursue them. . . .

"Our loss was 7,000, of which 4,000 English were killed and wounded. The Fusilier Brigade lost 54 officers and 1,100 men out of 1,500. The French losses were 1,000 prisoners, 3,000 killed and, if we are to believe intercepted letters, 5,000 wounded arrived at Seville.

"Marshal Soult withdrew his army to Llerema, but Beresford, ignoring the completeness of the

ALBUERA

victory of Albuera, expected to be attacked again next day and in his despatch to Lord Wellington observed: 'If I am attacked, I hope I shall not survive such another terrible day'."

This battle is described more in detail because a strange mistake was made about the responsibility of the charge of the 4th Division which decided the fate of the battle, which mistake is to the present day repeated in accounts of the event. When General Cole and his Staff were anxiously watching the fruitless attempts to storm the hill, the 4th Division being held in reserve to await an order from Sir W. Beresford, Major Hardinge,[1] D.Q.M.G., with Colonel Rooke, suggested, even urged, that General Cole should move his Division to the assistance of the troops. Neither could *give* an order, only *convey* one from the Commander-in-Chief. Nor could they undertake the responsibility of acting without orders. General Cole perfectly realised that the fate of the battle hung on his decision and rose to the occasion, taking the very serious risk of acting without orders.

General Cole's own account was given in a letter to Lord Enniskillen, dated Elvas, May 21st, 1811:

"We have had a most severe action with Marshal Soult, in which the British have as usual borne the principal share and have suffered dreadfully. Near two-thirds are killed and wounded—an immense number of officers. My friend Houghton killed, Stewart and myself wounded—his is slight and

---

[1] Napier says that Hardinge gave the order on his own responsibility.

mine merely a flesh wound through the thigh and of no consequence. My poor gallant Richard [Magenis, his nephew] has lost his left arm, but is doing well. My two A.D.C.'s badly. Wade is doing well, Roverea not so well. Either of them would be a sad loss to me. Out of six who lived with me, five are wounded.

"My Division came up from before Badajos as the action commenced, and as I believe no one will deny saved the day, the issue of which at one time was very, very doubtful. So severe a combat has not, I believe, taken place this war. Those who were in Talavera and Egypt say that the fire was more tremendous than at either of them. I certainly never saw anything like it and hope I never shall. For particulars I must refer you to the Marshal's [Beresford's] letter, who no doubt will make the best of it—and he had need to do so! My Portuguese behaved admirably, so I believe did all the others. From what I saw of the Spaniards, I must say that their conduct was good.[1] Very little of our Cavalry was engaged, the enemy's being so much superior.

"Lord Wellington arrived here the day before yesterday, to the general satisfaction of everybody. I expect to join the army in ten days or a fortnight."

Sir Charles Broke Vere, Assistant-Quartermaster-General of the 4th Division, who served with the Division from 1810 to 1812, gives the following account:

"General Cole continued anxiously to watch the progress of the contest, and he sent his A.D.C. to

---

[1] Napier is severe on them.

Sir W. Beresford to request authority to carry his Division to the support of the troops engaged. Colonel Rooke, D.A.G., and also Major Hardinge, Deputy-Quartermaster-General, had suggested, and the latter strongly urged on the General, the necessity of his advancing to reinforce the 2nd Division, but they brought no order from Sir W. Beresford, neither did his A.D.C. return with any answer.

"General Cole was impatient with being compelled to withhold support under an evident demand for succour, and at length the critical state of the conflict seemed to be so great that he took upon himself the responsibility of moving his Division to reinforce the battle without receiving any order from his superior to do so."

Lastly there is this letter from Lieut.-Col. H. Hardinge to Lowry Cole.

ALMENDALIGO
"MY DEAR GENERAL, *May* 24*th*, 1811
I write the very first spare moment I have found most sincerely to express my hopes that your wound will not have any troublesome consequences and that your fellow-sufferers in the dangers and glories of the day—Wade, Roverea and Egerton—are going on well. The first we are all very anxious to hear of and that he will not lose his arm, and that all of you may enjoy your reputation with sound limbs and health.

The Fuziliers exceeded anything the usual word gallantry can convey, and your movement on the left flank of the enemy unquestionably saved the day and decided the victory. Without considering the total numbers on each side, but merely the numbers in action at the point of contact, it must be admitted that our 6,000 British fought more desperately and bravely than anything that has as yet taken place in the Peninsula, and the enemy in conduct very dangerously rivalled them.

The enemy is at the foot of the Sierra Morena and all quiet to our front. His loss can by intercepted letters be ascertained to amount to 8,000 men, and probably the truth may lie nearer 10,000, so that your brave fellows did not fall unrevenged!

The Marshal and his Hd. Qrs. are very anxious to hear of you.

Your very faithful and sincere,
W. H. Hardinge"

CHAPTER VI

SALAMANCA

IN 1811 Wellington's pursuit of Masséna stopped in front of Ciudad Rodrigo, where the French leader, having received reinforcements, attempted to strike back in order to save Almeida from recapture by the British. The tactically somewhat indecisive battle of Fuentes d'Onor, however, immediately checked his effort, and Almeida again passed into British hands.

Thus both in the north and south Wellington's hold on Portugal was again secure by the middle of the year.

Rumours that Napoleon would organise another attempt on the country proved unfounded; he was, in fact, already preparing for his Russian campaign and was beginning to withdraw troops from the Peninsula.

So far Wellington in his defence of Portugal had made only short incursions into Spain; but an opportunity for a more ambitious campaign in 1812 was now presented by the weakening of the French armies and their dispersion, necessitated partly by the action of the Spanish guerillas, but even more by the difficulty of obtaining supplies in a country bled white by the army of occupation.

Wellington also had supply difficulties, but during the autumn and winter of 1811 he worked hard to improve his communications with the sea in order to facilitate concentration for the coming campaign. All the same his troops suffered great hardships and there was much sickness. Cole was one of the sufferers and was invalided to England.

Perhaps he was fortunate in this, as he thereby escaped the sieges of Ciudad Rodrigo and Badajoz, which terminated on January 19th and April 7th, 1812, respectively. The capture of these two fortresses was an essential preliminary to Wellington's projected operations against the French field armies, but they were desperately costly. Ciudad Rodrigo had been a slaughter, Badajoz a shambles, and what the Fourth Division had suffered in them is shown in a letter written by Cole to Lord Enniskillen when he rejoined the army:

LISBON
"MY DEAR E.,   5th June, 1812
I arrived here after a passage of 16 days from Portsmouth. My stay will, I hope, be short. I am anxious to join the army as it is believed they are on the move. . . .

I am once more embarked in the business, and if I keep my health and present resolution shall not quit it till it is over. But I will not answer for what change a year or two's separation from those I love best in the world may make in these sentiments. The fact is, I nearly despair of being able to gratify the first wish of my heart, viz. to be able to settle and live comfortably near you all. . . .

I have lost almost every friend and every good officer with at least a third of the Division at the siege of Badajos.

Your affte. Bro.
LOWRY COLE"

SALAMANCA

Previous to this Wellington's plan had taken definite shape. There were four main French armies to be taken into account: one keeping open communications in the north which was fully engaged with guerillas; Joseph's central reserve at Madrid; Soult in the south-west, who had failed to save Badajoz and who was kept anxious by the presence of detachments in that area. Finally in the north-west there was Marmont, who had succeeded Masséna in the Salamanca area.

It was against the last-named that Wellington had decided to strike, having first, by a bold use of Hill's detachment, destroyed the bridge of boats over the Tagus at Almarez; thus rendering it more difficult for Soult to reinforce either Joseph or Marmont, as all permanent bridges had been destroyed in Franco-Spanish fighting.

Wellington had to give his troops time to recover from their efforts in taking the fortresses and it was not till June 12th that his advance commenced in earnest. On the 17th he crossed the Tormes, and invested Salamanca, which had been fortified. Marmont himself manœuvred in the neighbourhood but could not prevent the capture of the place, which was completed on June 26th.

A vivid picture of the entry into Salamanca while the French garrison were still holding out in the forts is given in a letter from Captain George Bowles, a close friend of the Harris family, and (after Cole's marriage) of the Cole family too. It is addressed to Mrs. Robinson, aunt to Frances Harris:

MEMOIRS OF SIR LOWRY COLE

Camp near SALAMANCA
June 18th, 1812

"We arrived at this far-famed city at daybreak yesterday morning. Marshal Marmont, having withdrawn his outposts, advanced a few hours before, leaving however 600 Infantry in two strong forts commanding the bridge over the Tormes. This was apparently done with the intention of delaying our advance for a day or two. They still hold out, though we have one Division, the 6th, quartered in the town, as well as Headquarters, etc. We forded the river in places above and below the town and the whole army, consisting of about 36,000 effective Infantry and 4,000 Cavalry (exclusive of Spaniards) are on the north bank.

What Lord Wellington's further plans may be no one but himself knows. Our only difficulty is the want of bread, as if we advance further from our magazines the distance must oblige us to depend on the resources of the country, which, from the length of time the enemy has occupied it, cannot be very abundant, and must moreover be paid for in ready money.

The forts and their garrisons will be in our possession in a few hours. The wish of Lord Wellington not to waste lives has alone prevented it hitherto. Our mercy at Ciudad Rodrigo and Badajos is the cause of our being bullied by 500 men! . . .

I have just returned from seeing Salamanca, which, in spite of the residence of the French in it for nearly three years, still retains most of its former beauty. It is by far the finest city I have seen in this country. The convents, or rather colleges, twenty-five in number, are in general magnificent—at

SALAMANCA

least their outsides are, their insides being completely gutted by their late masters. The cathedral is superb and was reserved as a *bonne bouche* by his Excellency the Duke of Ragusa,[1] and our abrupt arrival alone prevented this design from being carried into execution.

It is almost impossible to describe the enthusiasm of our reception. Lord Wellington was in great danger of being smothered by the crowds of women who aspired to the honour of not only seeing but, I believe, kissing his Excellency. The nunneries were all thrown open and the repeated shouts of *'Viva los Ingleses'* have almost made my head ache."

When Salamanca finally passed into Wellington's hands Marmont retired behind the Douro. Wellington followed, but with the river high could not risk a crossing in the face of strong opposition. He waited some days hoping that lack of supplies would force a further retirement on his opponent, but Marmont held on and other troops were coming to his assistance. It was Wellington who now had to fall back from an exposed position which Joseph's army, threatening from Madrid, made precarious. Marmont forced the issue by initiating on July 15th movements to out-manœuvre Wellington. The rapid manœuvres of the next few days need not be described as they are famous in military history. Wellington fell back endeavouring to cover Salamanca and the road to Ciudad Rodrigo, and had somewhat the worst of it in the business of manœuvre, partly owing to the unreliability of his Spanish allies. The decisive moment finally came

---

[1] Marmont's title.

on July 22nd, when, after both armies had crossed the Tormes and Wellington had determined to continue his retirement to Portugal, Marmont attempted directly to oppose him. The moment for the supreme master of tactics had arrived, and, as it has been put, 40,000 men were disastrously defeated in forty minutes. Having his right and centre strongly posted, Marmont made the fatal mistake in his preliminary moves of attempting a too wide outflanking movement with his left in order to seize the Ciudad Rodrigo road. Wellington leapt at his chance, destroyed Marmont's exposed wing, and after a fierce struggle defeated the remainder of the army.

The 4th Division played an important part and Cole was severely wounded in the battle. The Division was posted on the Arapile hill, the key-point of the British right and the pivot round which the counter-attack was launched. Both defensively and in the counter-stroke the Division was in the thick of the action.

The 4th Division held one of the two important positions in the battlefield, two isolated crags which rose abruptly from the plain, known as Hermanitos. The other was occupied by the French. So important did Wellington consider the possession of this hill that, on one of his visits to the post, he told the Commanding Officer that he must defend the position to the last man. It was here or in the neighbouring village that Generals Cole, Leith and Sir William Beresford were badly wounded. The story is told in a letter from Colonel Wade, Cole's chief Staff officer, to Lord Grantham:

SALAMANCA

"My dear Lord Grantham,

Salamanca
24th July, 1812

I have much satisfaction in informing you that our dear General is doing as well as possible. He was severely wounded in the action of Salamanca, fought on the 22nd, leading on his Division to storm the heights occupied by the enemy. A musquet ball struck him a little below the left shoulder, broke the rib and passed out through the breast-bone—the lungs are very slightly touched. The surgeon who attends him, whose opinion experience has taught us to value, says he has every hope of his recovery. All the symptoms are favourable. He does not suffer much pain and has no fever. Indeed, from what Guthrie says, I have no doubt he will be restored to us. His spirits are very good as is his constitution. You shall hear as constantly as possible of the state of his health. He would himself write, but the position he is obliged to remain in prevents him.

We had a very severe action and gained what I hope the English will allow to be a complete victory. Marmont wished to turn our right and had his Divisions strongly posted on a ridge completely commanding all points by which we could attack. As soon as Lord Wellington observed his intentions, he attacked his left, which he turned with the 3rd Division led by General Pakenham. This front was immediately attacked in the most gallant manner by the 4th and 5th Divisions led by our brave General and General Leith, both of whom were wounded. In a very few minutes we drove them in at all points with their right Division at right angles to their former right to cover their retreat. This was attacked by the 6th Division and our Fusilier Brigade. The enemy was again obliged to give way and the rout became universal. Lord Wellington followed them on the Alba de Tormes road with the first and light Divisions. The fruits of this victory are 2 eagles, 19 pieces of artillery and about 10,000 men, 4,000 of whom are prisoners; the rest killed or wounded. Our loss, I should think, didn't exceed 3,000. I should think our Division had nearly 15,000 men opposed to it. Our Portuguese Brigade was outflanked and their left obliged to give way. However, they soon recovered.

I trust, my Lord, I shall be able to send you a more satisfactory account by the next mail of our good General. He is now asleep. We have him comfortably lodged in town."

By September 2nd Lowry Cole, in hospital at Salamanca, was able to write to Lady Grantham:

"I still continue to mend and hope in three weeks to commence my journey to Madrid in whose environs our army—at least the greater part of it—still are.

"The effects of our battle have begun to show themselves as Soult is certainly preparing to evacuate Andalusia. This, if there is any energy or talent in the government, will be of the greatest consequence, as it will give them country and resources to form an army. But I really begin to despair of ever seeing a tolerable Spanish regular army, though I by no means despair of driving the French utterly out of the country. If the Russians can occupy them for any time! . . .

SALAMANCA

"The enthusiasm with which Lord Wellington was received at Madrid, as I am told, is beyond belief. They cut pieces off the skirts of his coat to keep as relics, and women of the first rank ran into the streets and embraced the soldiers. You may imagine what the behaviour of the French must have been to cause such conduct. And yet they have their admirers even in our army! I am not, however, among them.

"I hope our friend Peel will like his new situation[1] of which I have many doubts, as the jobbing system still goes on there, I fear. The machinations are as strong as ever, and I am mistaken in him if he will willingly accede to them. I am sorry the negotiations with Canning are off. How the government will do without him I know not. Time will show.

"Your affte and attached brother,
"G. L. C."

In a letter to Lord Enniskillen, dated September 4th, 1812, he writes:

"The handsome manner in which Lord Wellington speaks of the conduct of the 4th Division unquestionably gives me great pleasure. But, believe me, the satisfaction it appears to give you gives me still greater. Lord W. still speaks of their conduct as the best he had ever witnessed. It certainly could not have been more gallant...."

Even after the brilliant victory of Salamanca and the victorious march on Madrid, the allies could

---

[1] As Chief Secretary in Ireland.

not yet hold their conquests in Spain. Soult was approaching from Andalusia and Wellington, after an unsuccessful attempt to bring Marmont's army (now commanded by Clausel) to action, was obliged to withdraw once more into Portugal. Cole rejoined during this withdrawal, and describes some of its episodes in a letter to Lady Grantham:

S. Joao de Pequiera
13th December, 1812

"My dearest Henrietta,

I have to thank you for three letters . . . and the last without a date announcing my return for Fermanagh, for all of which I thank you from my heart and could wish any one individual of my family was half as kind in thinking or writing to me as you have been, and for which I really feel grateful. . . .

It is now, if it were not so before, evident that being a soldier is the best recommendation a Fermanagh candidate can have. It was rather a singular circumstance that my colleague—and we presume my adversary—should both want an arm! I hope when I present myself I shall have both mine!

I believe I wrote you a few lines from Ciudad Rodrigo the day I arrived there after our retreat from the Tormes [river], which was by far the severest lesson I ever experienced in my military career, and I believe the severest any British troops have experienced this war—Sir John Moore's retreat excepted! Fortunately it didn't last long and the enemy, being, I believe, very glad to get rid of us without a fight, did not press us. Otherwise we should have lost a good many men, as we did some

SALAMANCA

by straggling. The weather was uncommonly severe, some of us ill off for bread, among these the 4th Division, and the troops suffered much. I really never saw so much misery as in the few days between the 15th and the 19th November.

General Hill having requested me to take the rear guard, which consisted of my own and the Light Division and three Brigades of Cavalry, I was, to begin with, between the hours of ten in the morning of the 30th until five o'clock on the evening of the 31st, either on foot or horseback and almost without eating. I had only joined the Division the previous night and had at the time no idea I was equal to the Fagg. I have, however, not suffered in the least from it, except that perhaps my wound, which is still open though almost closed, might perhaps have been healed. Be that as it may, I should have been sorry to have been absent at the time, and as to my health, I am even better than I have been, so it is of no consequence. . . .

The army has dispersed and are now in cantonments for the winter if the enemy do not molest us, which I hope and should suppose they will not. All ranks are in want of a little respite from fatigue to recruit the animal as well as physical strength and recover from the effects of a campaign of nearly a year—I might almost say ever since Masséna first entered this country, now upwards of two years. For if we were on the march we were almost constantly in sight of the enemy. The 4th Division have had a full share of the Fagg as well as the glory of it, and I believe and think have done their duty as well as any other. Between ourselves and Grantham, they have lost in killed and wounded alone upwards of 5,000, upwards of 250 of whom were officers, including those who have been twice and thrice wounded, of which there are many. . . .

John Bull, who is ever too much depressed or elated according to circumstances, will, I fear, prevent the present Ministry, if so inclined, from carrying on the war on its present scale, the only one on which we can hope to drive the enemy out of the Peninsula. That is to say, if Russia, which I hope it may do by occupying Bonaparte on the north, can prevent France from sending any considerable reinforcements to this country.

Lord Wellington has, I believe, left Freneda for Cadiz. It is to be hoped he will stimulate the government there to some exertion. . . .

The people still continue our friends and their hatred of the French, notwithstanding I regret to say that our troops committed, I think, even more destruction in the retreat than they are in the habit of doing; the peasantry still continue to find and send on to us any of our prisoners who escape from the enemy.

I should certainly have been very glad if we could have wintered in Spain, as the accommodation and cleanness of the villages there is even in the extreme superior to Portugal.

I am personally very well off for this country, but there are no fireplaces and the house is too good to spoil by making a temporary one. I think, however, I shall have to make the attempt, as I am really so cold at this moment that I can scarcely hold the pen. Although the weather is far from cold, this is by far the coldest country I ever saw. From the inroads of the enemy and from our own depredations,

SALAMANCA

there is scarce anything to be procured except bread and beef, which commissary provides us. I shall therefore, my love, if I hadn't sufficient without them, have other reasons to regret not passing the winter with you, viz. the luxury of your table, to which I begin to find I am not indifferent as I used to be.

In Spain those unknown creatures women are really the ugliest and fattest I have ever seen. I shall have likewise therefore to regret the society of some of your pretty friends! By the bye, talking of them, I saw in a magazine that Alfred Harris is married to one of the Miss Markhams. If she is the one you introduced me to in London, I think he has made a good choice.

G. L. C."

If, as is probable, he was thinking of a special pretty friend of his sister's, it is satisfactory to know that she was also thinking of him. Here is a letter from Lord Grantham's brother, Frederick Robinson (afterwards Lord Goderich), who was at the Admiralty and favourite secretary to Lord Castlereagh. He says in answer to enquiries by Catherine Harris (sister to Frances):

August 20th, 1812

"I would have obeyed your commands to write to you to Edinburgh, but in the absence of any official confirmation of the victory of Salamanca during the time you expected to be at that place, I thought I might as well wait till I should be sure of your having reached Scone. And as the news arrived on Sunday, I had no means of anticipating the Gazette which will have conveyed to you as much as I could have done.

Nothing, I think, could be more complete than this great and important victory, the most brilliant and decisive that the British army has gained for centuries. I understand on unquestionable authority that up to the 28th July the total loss of the enemy is not overstated at 17,000 men, and the moral effect of such a smash upon the debris of Marmont's army must render it altogether inefficient for a considerable length of time.

I wish we could catch hold of King Joseph, who seems to be in some jeopardy as Lord Wellington appears to have placed himself between his corps and that of Marmont. I can almost pity Joseph, who I believe is heartily sick of its regal honours and sighs for the ease of a more humble life.

Great rejoicings have taken place in London and we have been plagued with illuminations for three nights. Lord Wellesley did not think it undignified to drive about the streets in his chariot and receive the applause of the mob, who with their fickleness were greatly delighted with the good news and broke some of Burdett's windows, forgetting that two years ago they had broken the windows of half the houses in town in order to do honour to the said Baronet's unworthy escape.

Our loss is surprisingly small and I have peculiar pleasure in being able to say that Lowry Cole is doing as well as possible."

[The writer then quoted the account of Cole's condition as described in Colonel Wade's letter to Lord Grantham, and continued:]

SALAMANCA

"This good report has been a great relief to Lady Grantham, who was extremely agitated for twenty-four hours between the first mention of his wound in Trant's letter from Oporto and the arrival of the despatches.

So much for others; now for myself. You may have seen in the papers that I am become a Privy Councillor. The fact is so and I am to be Vice President of the Board of Trade. It is an office without a salary but with a considerable share of business. I am obliged therefore to retain my situation at the Admiralty...."

It was proper that Lowry Cole's gallantry should be acknowledged, as it was in March 1813, by the conferring on him of the K.C.B., and the honour was enhanced by the manner of its announcement:

"The Duke of Wellington
    to General Lowry Cole.

FRENEDA
March 7th, 1813
5 P.M.

MY DEAR COLE,

The post has just arrived and brought the enclosed letters to announce that you are made Knight of the Bath, of which I received an intimation some time ago. I beg leave to congratulate you on this well-deserved honour. The box containing the Insignia is here and I will invest you with them with the greatest satisfaction on any day you will fix upon to come over here. We are not very roomy at Freneda, but we ought to have present the General, Officers and Staff of your Division and some of the Commanding Officers of regiments. I am not quite certain if it would not be best to inform headquarters at Ciudad Rodrigo for the occasion.

Ever yours most sincerely,
WELLINGTON"

CHAPTER VII

THE BATTLES OF THE PYRENEES

ENCOURAGED by Wellington's success in 1812 and by Napoleon's difficulties, the British Government sent strong reinforcements to the Peninsula, and the Spanish armies also became a more important factor, partly from restored morale and still more from having been placed under Wellington's command. The French armies had correspondingly deteriorated both in numbers and confidence. Thus in 1813 Wellington for the first time enjoyed a position of superiority. If he advanced against the main line of communication of the French they must fight or withdraw from the country. Either course accorded with Wellington's desire and consequently he could afford to be satisfied by manœuvring to turn the French out of positions too strong for decisive attack and to wait for a more favourable opportunity to seek a decision. In consequence, though the campaign began in May it was not till June 21st that the decisive battle was fought at Vittoria; Joseph, now commanding the main French army, had hoped to hold the line of the Douro, but his position was turned and he fell back on the Ebro. Here his position was again turned, but his main line of retreat was cut and he was forced to fight at a disadvantage and his overthrow was complete. This battle practically marked the end of the Peninsular War, though for a short period Wellington, in what we know as the Battles of the Pyrenees, had to resist attempts by Soult (who superseded Joseph in command) to retrieve the situation and relieve the fortresses of Pampeluna and San Sebastian, still holding out. Following on the failure of Soult's counter-stroke came the invasion of France and much hard fighting, ending with the battle of Toulouse on April 10th, the day before the provisional Treaty of Paris was signed.

For the whole of this campaign we have to depend on Lowry Cole's own letters, which are meagre in detail and often written under great difficulties and when he was almost worn out with fatigue. There are no more diaries of Major Roverea to refer to, for he was killed about July 28th in the Battle of Sauroren, one of the actions during the battles of the Pyrenees. Lowry Cole had made a great friend of his A.D.C., and since the Swiss could not of course go home when on leave, the General commended him to his own relations, with whom Roverea stayed in their country houses.

In the Battle of Vittoria Cole's Division was hotly engaged and he himself and his Portuguese Brigade were specially mentioned in Wellington's despatches. Evidently Cole agreed that his Portuguese had distinguished themselves, as appears from his letter to his sister Lady Florence Balfour:

<blockquote>
7 Leagues from PAMPELUNA
on the road from Vittoria
24th June, 1813
</blockquote>

"MY DEAREST FOFF,

I have only time to say I am well and untouched after the most brilliant victory we have

THE BATTLES OF THE PYRENEES

ever obtained over the enemy. None of my Staff hurt. The Division behaved as usual very well and my Portuguese Brigade admirably. In fact, nothing could have been more gallant than their conduct. We are in full march for Pampeluna, which report says wants provisions. It is hard to say what may be the consequences of this victory. I am sanguine enough to hope to see *real France*.

P.S.—The first halt we have I will write, but for God's sake do not fall into old habits of neglecting me."

This letter, it will be seen, was written when Cole was on his way to Pampeluna, and the part he took in covering the investment of that fortress against Soult's efforts to relieve it was perhaps the most brilliant episode in his career, for he was there in a position of greater independence and responsibility. But the intricate story of the Battles of the Pyrenees belongs to military history and cannot be followed in a personal memoir. It suffices to quote the Duke's commendation of the behaviour of the 4th Division:

"In the course of this action, the gallant Fourth Division, which has been so frequently distinguished in this army, surpassed their former good conduct. It is impossible to describe the enthusiastic bravery of the Fourth Division, and I was very much indebted to Sir Lowry Cole for the manner in which he directed their operations, to Major-General Anson, Major-General Ross, Major-General Byng and Brigadier-General Campbell, of the Portuguese service. All the officers commanding and the officers of the regiments were remarkable for their gallantry."

Cole himself wrote:

> *August 4th*, 1813
> ESCHALAZ, on the Frontier of Spain
>
> "I am so completely tired that I have not time to say more than that I am in good health and have escaped untouched after seven days' fighting, some of which were very severe. The Division has suffered severely, but has gained great credit.
>
> I have, I regret to say, lost my valuable friend Roverea, who was shot in the head on the 28th. Such is the fate of war! I felt it hard to part with one who had been almost constantly with me for upwards of eight years, and for whom I had a sincere affection which I believe he returned.
>
> Wade[1] is perfectly well as are all my Staff. God bless you, my love, and believe me to remain,
>
> Your affec^{ate} Brother,
> G. LOWRY COLE"

For several weeks the Division was cantoned at Lisaca on the Bidassoa, and on August 9th Cole wrote from there to Lady Grantham:

"MY DEAREST NET,
    I wrote you a few lines after out late hard-fought and brilliant victory. I do not know what John Bull will say to it, but the Army here ranks it first among those in the Peninsula. I have a strong interest to think so, as almost the whole of it fell on the 4th Division. Nothing could be finer than their conduct throughout and Lord Wellington speaks of nothing else. I am satisfied for this year and hope most sincerely they will let us alone for the re-

---

[1] His senior staff officer.

THE BATTLES OF THE PYRENEES

mainder of the campaign, at least until Pampeluna and San Sebastian fall. I shall thank Grantham to send me Arrowsmith's map of the Pyrenees. . . .

About a month later he wrote again:

LISACA
4th September

"MY DEAREST NET,

I have received your letter of the 13th August, and, believe me, Net, the greatest satisfaction I feel in the *praise* which Lord Wellington gives, and gives *justly*, to the Division is that which it affords my friends. I do not at the same time mean to say that I do not feel a great deal of personal pride on the occasion. Lord Wellington still continues to speak of the conduct on that day as the finest he ever witnessed. And he wrote to Sir Thomas Graham saying he had never seen troops behave so well.

The two days previous I had a good deal of mental as well as personal Fagg, and if you knew what difficulties we Generals of Divisions occasionally have when separated,[1] you would not think our situation enviable. All's well that ends well, and so has this been. And I consider myself most particularly fortunate at all times, but particularly so on the present occasion.

You will see in the papers that Marshal Soult has again attacked us, and has again been defeated. One of my Brigades only was engaged, and that detached from me. The principal share fell to the Spanish army, who behaved admirably. I was close to them and saw the whole of it. I have seldom seen more gallantry. This gives me particular satisfac-

[1] That is, on detached duty.

tion, as it takes away one of the principal arguments from the Croakers who used to say they would never be any good.

I have received the map of the Pyrenees, for which I thank you. And pray tell Grantham that I feel both thankful and proud of his anxiety about me as a proof of his regard!

I must now conclude as the Packet is about to be closed—which I hope the campaign will also do. The town of San Sebastian is taken and I hope the Castle will soon follow. Our loss has been tremendous for such a thing.

I feel there is no chance of my seeing you this winter. If I can, I will. My friends Murray and Stewart are to be made K.C.B.'s, which gives me great satisfaction. Pakenham [Sir Edward] took it into his head that I should have got a Peerage, but there are, if they were inclined to it at home, too many in my way for me to think of it. If there was a peace, I should like to succeed Cradock at the Cape for a few years, as I am told one may live 'en Prince' and save a good deal of cash. The only thing is to live among you *creditable*. I hope you have received my letter to Arthur."

To Lord Enniskillen.

Vera (Spain)
30th October, 1813

"The 4th Division has not yet entered France, but we expect to do so on the fall of Pampeluna, which is daily expected. If the enemy show no more pluck than they did in our last attack, it will be an easy enough business. But I wish it was not thought necessary to enter France, as I fear we shall have troublesome winter quarters. God grant that this winter may put an end to the war and give us peace on fair terms."

On October 31st Pampeluna fell and Wellington was free to move forward. The news from Germany was encouraging—fresh disasters to the Grande Armée and Napoleon's power crumbling away. The winter weather in the mountains and the hardships from cold and wet endured by his soldiers, who were often insufficiently clothed, made it very necessary to bring them to less exposed regions. Both armies suffered from want of supplies and the British thought longingly of better cantonments in France. Soult had made tremendous preparations for defence, which stretched from St. Jean Pied du Port to Bayonne. The left of his position lay on the heights behind the right bank of the river, separated from the rest of the army by the gorge of the Amotz, where the Nivelle changes its course from north to west and sweeps in an arc alongside of the positions occupied by Clausel in the centre and Reille on the right of the French line. The centre extended from Amotz along a steep mountain crest as far as the village of Ascain.

Marshal Beresford, who commanded three Divisions (British), the 3rd, the 7th, and the 4th, was ordered to dislodge Clausel from his fortified mountain and by driving him across the river to lay Reille's left flank and rear open to attack. On Clausel's right front rose the rocky eminence of the Petite Rhune, which he held as an earthwork on his left front, a ridge separated his main position from the village of Sarre, the approach to which was covered by strong redoubts.

A despatch from Sir Lowry Cole gives an official account of the fighting that followed. A private letter adds criticism.

To Lord Enniskillen.

13*th November*, 1813
Camp in front of BOIS DE ST. PEE
"MY DEAREST E.,
I must as usual refer you to the Gazette for an account of our proceedings of late. All my Staff and self have escaped unhurt. The Division behaved with their usual gallantry and I hope will hold their usual proper place in the Gazette. This will all go to the credit of Marshal Sir William Beresford, who, proposing to go home this winter and wishing to go there with *éclat*, asked for a command. Lord Wellington, not knowing how to refuse him, to my great annoyance gave him the nominal command of three Divisions, the 3rd, 4th and 7th—nominal, for we received our orders direct from the Quarter-master General, and the Marshal never gave me an order during the action. His aim is no doubt a peerage, to which I have no objection if he does not continue in command of the 4th Division...."

Cole's official account of that battle of the Nivelle, addressed to Marshal Beresford, will be found in Appendix C, being too detailed for the general reader. But a glance at it will show how generously he upheld the best army tradition of giving recognition to valour and ability in his

THE BATTLES OF THE PYRENEES

troops and subordinate officers, and in claiming it for them.

To his brother, Lord Enniskillen, he wrote on Christmas Day 1813 from Usteritz:

"I must begin by wishing you all the good wishes of the season. . . .

"My last letter was of the 4th December, since when we have had a good deal of Fagg and some hard fighting, but I was not engaged, and constant rains for this last week. We have been again sent to cantonments, how long to remain is hard to say, but I hope and think for some months. Mine are not very good, but we are under cover and anything is better than a hut in this weather. The inhabitants appear better pleased to have us than their own army. However, all armies must be a sad nuisance to the natives. All ranks are evidently dissatisfied with their government and governor, and I believe wish us to succeed. We cannot, however, expect any active exertion in our favour, but it is said that if we advance they will rise *en masse*. For the present, however, I see no immediate prospect of our passing the Adour.

"What I think appears to bear hardest on all ranks is the conscription. They appear a very quiet and orderly and comfortable peasantry, well lodged and the farms very neat. I wish there were any like them in our own country."

About a month later the Adour was crossed. This was a feat of arms in which the 4th Division had no share, but they bore the brunt, or at least played an important part, in the Battles of St. Boës and Orthez, and there was no harder fighting anywhere. Each combat was a gain to the Allies and brought the end nearer.

Soult, forced to retreat, took the road to Tarbes and Toulouse, leaving Bordeaux to its fate, which was very much according to the wishes of the citizens, for in this city the partisans of the Bourbons were in the majority.

After the victories of St. Boës and Orthez, the city sent a deputation and invitation to the Duke of Wellington at St. Jean du Luz. The Duc d'Angoulême,[1] who was also at the British headquarters, was invited to go to Bordeaux, and was escorted thither by Marshal Beresford. He was received by the Mayor wearing the white cockade, who handed over the keys of the city. The Imperial Governor withdrew with the garrison and the great French port was open to British commerce. Soult, having failed to get any help from Marshal Suchet in the Eastern Provinces, made his last stand at Toulouse.

Cole wrote to Lady Grantham:

GRENADA
"MY DEAREST NET,   3rd March, 1814

This is the first opportunity or time I have had to write a line since the battle of St. Boës near Orthez. The 4th Division as usual were principals and have suffered considerably. I have lost some valuable friends and good officers, but all my personal Staff escaped as well as myself. The total loss of our Army has not been very great. The enemy

---
[1] Married to the daughter of Louis XVI.

THE BATTLES OF THE PYRENEES

behaved much better than I have seen them do for a length of time, which was the less expected as we have been so much accustomed to drive them before us...."

To the same.

23rd March, 1814

"I have had since I wrote to you from Grenada to thank you for your letter of the 13th ult....

You will have heard probably by Lord Wellington's despatches of the march of the 4th and the 7th Divisions on Bordeaux. The former reached no further than Lanzon, which is eight leagues short of it and on the Garonne.

Thinking, however, that we might retrace our steps, I went there (to Bordeaux) with the intention of staying there a few days, but the very day I left the Division an order arrived for them to rejoin the Army. My stay, therefore, was very short. But, though short, it was very gratifying as this is one of the finest and best-built cities I have ever seen—almost everything to be had. I had not time, however, to do what I intended to do—to send my friends some claret, among whom Grantham would not have been forgotten. And I send you a lace shawl, which, if I am not grossly imposed upon, is of much greater value in England than the trifle I paid for it. For curiosity's sake I shall thank you to let me know what its value may be there! At all events, my love, if they are not of value, they will prove to you that even in my moments of recreation I think of you.

We commenced our march from Lanzon on the 15th and rejoined the Army on the 18th, and have never had a halt since. We are now in sight of Thoulouse and would probably be in possession of it to-morrow if it were not at the other side of the Garonne. The opinion of the people there, I hear, is as much in our favour as at Bordeaux, but, Soult being there with his whole army until we can get him out of it, they cannot declare themselves. Throughout the country we have been well received, but except at Bordeaux there has been no open declaration in favour of the Bourbons.

I am, much as I wish for peace, decidedly against our making peace with Bonaparte. If the Allies made this clear, I am convinced we would have three-fourths of the country in their favour."

On March 30th, 1814, Blücher and Schwartzenberg arrived in front of Paris with 200,000 men. Marshals Marmont and Mortier, who were charged with its defence, could not depend on more than 28,000. After an obstinate resistance and ten hours' fighting, they were defeated and the Emperor Alexander with the King of Prussia entered Paris. After various negotiations carried on between the Allies, a provisional government and Napoleon's emissaries, Napoleon at last realised that he was beaten and abdicated unconditionally at Fontainebleau on April 6th, 1814, this step having been rendered imperative by the desertion of Marmont and his army.

On April 10th, 1814, the Battle of Toulouse was fought, the British entered that city and the Peninsular War was ended.

On April 11th the provisional Treaty of Paris was signed and on April 20th Napoleon bade fare-

THE BATTLES OF THE PYRENEES

well to the Guard at Fontainebleau and started for Elba.

On April 24th Louis XVIII landed at Calais.

Lowry Cole wrote to Lady Enniskillen on April 16th:

LA BASTIDE
2 Leagues from Thoulouse

"Since the few lines I wrote you by Lord W. Russell, who went home with Lord Wellington's despatches, I have received yours of the 19th. . . . A very short time will, I hope, enable me to talk over them and other subjects in London, as the late unexpected events which have taken place in Paris give every reason to hope the war is at an end and a peace for our lifetime. God grant it! What a lesson it has been to ambition, and what a glorious unexpected end it is to the war! To me it is an additional satisfaction that on our part it has been terminated by a victory.

Nothing can be more fortunate than Lord Wellington's career has been. Mine in a much humbler sphere has been likewise very fortunate. And if I can scrape up enough to live upon and a mate to my choice, I shall not envy anyone! I believe with Solon that no one can be called fortunate till he is dead!

I am very undetermined as to my movements when I am at liberty—whether to go straight home or to make a tour via Lyons, Switzerland and Paris home.

What a glorious finale to the war! The most sanguine minds could not have looked to it a year ago.

Nett [Lady Grantham] wrote to me that you proposed going to London, so I hope I shall find you there when I arrive. What I shall do I know not, as my finances will be poor. I shall probably be obliged to live with you at Florence Court till you are tired of me."

CHAPTER VIII

THE PEACE OF PARIS

AFTER his return, Lowry Cole went home to Ireland, where he was greatly fêted—and rather embarrassed.

To Lady Grantham.

FLORENCE COURT
"MY DEAREST NET, *22nd October*, 1814
Enniskillen . . . wrote to you a few days ago enclosing the account of my reception by the gentlemen of the county. It was certainly flattering but sadly annoying! I am convinced Nature never intended me for a public character and the more I see of a quiet life the more I am desirous of settling down, or rather of having the means of doing so. My own little place[1] is tempting, and I dream of nothing but improvements. I will not answer how soon I may be guilty of retiring to it—if I can make my arrangements with Enniskillen respecting it. A *home* after all, as you say, embellishes everything.
I go on Thursday to Haslewood [his sister Lady Sarah Wynne's home] to meet Longford. Edward Pakenham is gone to England to attend Col. Quinton's court-martial. I shall not be surprised

---

[1] Marlbank, two miles from Blacklion on the Fermanagh side, looking north over Lough Macrean. It had been an outlying homefarm of the Enniskillen estate and is now a farmhouse of the occupying owner.

if he is sent out to America to assume the command poor Ross had. It would seem as if we had failed in Upper Canada. This may make a change in commanders there, and Lord Hill or Edward Paget be sent to supersede Sir George Prevost, as I believe the government were not satisfied with Sir George previously. I hope they may not offer any command to me and it is not likely they will. . . ."

Some notes are needed here, as the inglorious second American war is little known. Sir Edward Pakenham (brother to Lowry Cole's flame, Kitty, the Duchess of Wellington) commanded the 3rd Division in the Peninsula. He was sent now, as Cole guessed, to America, and on New Year's Day, 1815, was killed leading a disastrous attack on New Orleans. Ross, another Irishman, had distinguished himself first under Cole at Maida, where he led the 20th Regiment. He commanded a brigade in Cole's Fourth Division with great distinction. After the end of the war in France, four brigades of Wellington's army were sent to America, three to Canada, and one under Ross to act with the Navy against the coasts. Ross entered the Potomac, defeated a strong American force at Bladensburg, marched on Washington and burnt it. Next, directing himself against Baltimore, he was killed in some skirmishing on September 12th, 1814. His descendants bear the name Ross of Bladensburg.

Prevost had been Governor-General of British North America since 1811, and was in charge when the United States declared war on England on June 18th, 1812. The operations in Canada remained under his command, with disastrous

THE PEACE OF PARIS

results. Especially the troops sent on after the Peninsular service, among which were two battalions of the Inniskillings, resented fiercely his handling of them, and after a disgraceful failure at Plattsburg in September 1814, there was almost mutiny.

Sir Lowry's letters after his return to England are not so joyful as might have been expected. The old grievance against his sisters for neglecting to write to him reappears. He finds his prospects disappointing and his means insufficient. After all the perils and drain of war and the exciting finale of the two great victories which terminated the campaign, there must have come a reaction and it might be possible to find peace and inaction unsatisfying. What he really wanted was a home of his own.

Some years previously, when he met Lady Frances Harris at the house of her aunt Mrs. Robinson, in Wiltshire, he had fallen in love with her: but at that time he was on active service and also thought himself too poor to come forward. Now, until he had seen Lady Frances and settled plans with her for their future life, he was restless and unhappy, and apparently it took some months to do this.

It must, however, have been some offset to despondency when the Speaker in the House of Commons, tendering the thanks of Parliament to the Army, turned to where Sir Lowry Cole sat and addressed him personally in these words:

"In that victorious army which re-established the thrones of our allies, though all were brave, yet by the fortune of war the skill and valour of some were rendered conspicuous above the rest, and the gallant Fourth Division was distinguished throughout by the highest praise for its enthusiastic courage and heroic devotion. Of that Division to whom all eyes were turned, in every battle, you, Sir, had the chief command, and your growing renown was well supported by many brave companions in arms whose names will ever live in our annals."

Meanwhile the great world both in Paris and London was intoxicated with delight at the fall of the arch-enemy Napoleon, who had made life so difficult and uneasy for many years, and who was now on his way to Elba, followed across France by a hundred *fourgons* of possessions! Louis XVIII, for his part, was on his way to occupy the vacant throne. We are not told about his luggage. Many of his subjects welcomed him, no doubt, but to most of the nation he was acceptable only because they hoped his accession would secure peace. They had had more than enough honour and glory. He landed at Calais on April 24th, but did not enter Paris till May 2nd. Monsieur, the Comte d'Artois,[1] his brother, made an informal entry into the capital on April 11th. The following letter gives an account of this. It is from the Hon. Frederick Robinson (afterwards Lord Goderich) to his aunt, the Dowager Lady Grantham. This future Prime Minister was then a rising politician, vice-president of the Board of Trade; but at this time he was abroad accompanying Lord Castlereagh, who was in charge of the negotiations for the Peace of Paris.

[1] Afterwards Charles X.

THE PEACE OF PARIS

PARIS
April 12th, 1814

"DEAR AUNT,

A letter from Paris under our present circumstances will, I hope, make up for all former deficiencies. We had intended to have despatched a messenger yesterday, but the whole day and evening was occupied in one of the most striking and interesting sights I ever witnessed—*the entry of Monsieur into Paris!*

About eleven o'clock Castlereagh and I (*en grande tenue*) mounted our horses and joined the cavalcade that went out to meet him. The streets were crowded to the greatest degree and lined by the National Guard. At a little distance from the Barrière we drew up by the roadside to await his arrival. He was on horseback surrounded by officers of the National Guard and some of his own personal attendants. As soon as he saw Castlereagh, he called him up and we proceeded with the procession close to him. He was soon after met by the French Marshals, Kellerman, Moncey, Ney, Marmont, etc., and a mutual salutation took place which (although somewhat awkward from various circumstances) went off very well. The procession then proceeded to the Church of Notre Dame, where the Te Deum was sung. No words can describe the joy and enthusiasm of the innumerable crowds, who literally *paved* the streets. The women in particular showed the liveliest interest. I saw many in the windows and in the streets who were absolutely overcome and fainted from excess of feeling! In short, it exceeded all demonstrations of joy I ever saw.

In the evening the play of *La partie de chasse de*

Henri IV was revived at the Théâtre Français and the famous song in the last act of 'Vive Henri IV' was sung in chorus by the whole house standing up. At the conclusion of the play an impromptu was sung which had some very good points in it and was received with infinite applause.

I can scarcely believe that I am in Paris, the Bourbon restored and Bonaparte dethroned! But so it is, and I hope we shall stay here a little longer. I really could not give up Paris yet. I have not had time to see anything, and there is more to be seen here than in any capital in Europe! It is not, however, improbable that I may be obliged to go over to England for a short time if it is thought necessary that someone who has been a party to all that has occurred should attend to give explanations in the House. It is certainly much to be desired that Castlereagh should still continue here, and therefore I may perhaps be turned into his *double*. But it would only be a trip.

We expect Lady Castlereagh from Brussels as the road is quite open."

The following extract from Lady Malmesbury's diary gives an amusing sidelight on popular feeling in Paris in 1814:

"I dined at Monsieur de la Coste's. Gabriel de Vérac very entertaining with his account of the extreme insouciance of the Parisians the day Paris was taken in 1814 by the Prussian army under Blücher and the Russian army. He said that on the boulevards everything was in *statu quo*—the ladies in their *calèches*, the gentlemen on horseback flirting

with them. '*Qu'est-ce qui arrive? Belleville est prise—
et dans une demie-heure ce sera fini. Bon jour, Madame.*'
And this indifference, although the wounded were
being carried in on one side and on the other all
the usual train of *promeneurs*, of dancing dogs,
escamoteurs and the mobs round them. The cafés
full of people lounging, eating their meals and
reading the papers. A man coming in says, '*Eh
bien, dans une demi-heure la ville est prise! Donnez-moi
une côtelette.*'
The next morning he saw a crowd at a baker's
shop in the Rue du Bac. The Russians had come in
the night before. The baker was swearing at them
and abusing them, and upon Gabriel's enquiring
why he did so:
'*Mais, Monsieur, ces gueux-là m'ont pris tout mon
pain.*'
'*Comment! Ils vous l'ont pris? Est-ce qu'ils ne vous
l'ont pas payé?*'
'*Comment, Monsieur! Je voudrais bien voir cela qu'ils
ne me l'eussent pas payé!*'
Certainly they are the most extraordinary
people!"

We have had a glimpse of Lady Malmesbury
when she was a young woman travelling in Italy
with her husband and enjoying herself to the
utmost as the centre of a gay society of young men
on the grand tour, and pleasure-seeking English
friends like herself, just before the outbreak of
war with France, which, except for a few short intervals, closed Europe to English travellers for many
years. To judge by her diaries, she was very much
interested in public affairs and rather inclined to

take a hand in the game herself. Her gossip is always political. She never alludes to the appearance or clothes of her own friends or of the many notabilities she is continually meeting—always to their politics. She was detached and independent in her views, an outspoken woman, telling the unvarnished truth even to kings. . . . Society and the many friends she found there were all-important to her. To Park Place, near Henley, where the Malmesburys lived for some years after they left Brookwood, came a constant stream of friends and intimates, such as Lord and Lady Bathurst, Lord and Lady Pembroke from Wilton, with Russians, French and Dutch under her auspices.

While Lord Malmesbury and his wife were in Russia, they were a good deal separated from their children, who were confided to the care of a family friend, Miss Cozens. In due course the two boys went to school and the girls, Catherine and Frances, remained in her care at Brookwood in Hampshire, where their father had a small country place. The long absences of their parents were bridged over by letters much valued by the children. Frances kept all hers from her father, whom she evidently adored. Miss Cozens's care was supplemented by that of Lord Malmesbury's sisters, Miss Harris and Mrs. Robinson; and Durnford, their home in Wiltshire, was a great centre for the young people of the family. So the Harris children grew up with their cousins, Lord Minto's family, and with the Temples, for Lady Palmerston was a great friend of Lady Malmesbury, while George and William Bowles, wards of Lord Malmesbury, were like brothers to them. Not to mention the little

French refugee, Caroline de Noailles, whose nurse brought her over in a fishing boat to England after her mother, the Comtesse de Noailles, had perished on the scaffold with the Duchesse de Grammont and Madame d'Ayen. Lady Malmesbury says in her diary that she very nearly adopted her.

Her daughters, Lady Catherine and Lady Frances, became accomplished women of the world, but I cannot help thinking that the formation of their character was the work of Miss Cozens and their aunts.

No letters from Lady Malmesbury to her daughter are preserved; that may be accidental, but I suspect that she was not an easy, amiable person, but one to be reckoned with. In 1815 Lady Frances shows in her letters how anxious she was as to her mother's reception of the match, suitable as most people would have thought it. But although Lady Malmesbury declared her wish that neither of her daughters should marry a soldier or an Irishman, she became very fond of Sir Lowry.

Lady Frances was thirty-two at the time of her marriage—just the right age, one would think, for Sir Lowry, who was forty-two, but not according to the views of his friend, that rough warrior, Sir Thomas Picton, who opined that, for his part, if he had been such a fool as to marry at Cole's age, he would have been a d——d fool and have married the youngest woman he could find.

What was Lady Fanny doing at this moment of great events? The letters from her side of the family must take up the story. If we had only Sir Lowry's to depend on, this chronicle would be very dull.

Though a man of many noble qualities and a very fine soldier, he was far from being an interesting correspondent. On principle he was too discreet. Nor had he a lively fancy or a literary style to enable him to present his facts picturesquely.

Lady Fanny was then paying her aunt Mrs. Robinson a visit in town at her house in Privy Gardens, near Richmond Terrace, Whitehall, in hopes of seeing something of the Peace rejoicings and the welcome of the English people to the King of France and the allied sovereigns.

"Little Aunt Robinson", as she was called in her family circle, deserves consideration in this medley of papers, not only because she was a great letter-writer and so attracted letters from all sorts of people, but also from her habit of collecting every scrap of information—gossip, if you like—political and social, going about the town, and of copying it out. For this she had ample opportunity, being one of those women who had always lived in political circles and there found herself in her element.

She knew European society almost as well as English, having passed months with her brother, Lord Malmesbury, when as Sir James Harris he was ambassador at St. Petersburg. There she made many Russian friends, and if one may judge from the letters preserved had quite a place of her own in that distant capital. The journey there was disagreeable and sometimes attended with danger, but, nothing daunted, she travelled out alone with her maid to join her brother and sister-in-law and was wrecked somewhere in the Baltic, but without any serious consequences.

At the time of Lady Frances's marriage she was a

THE PEACE OF PARIS

widow, elderly, still devoted to society and entertainment and as eager as ever to see all the sights and meet all the people of importance, quite a personage in her own way. Most kind and hospitable to her nephews and nieces and other young connections, she was ever ready to help them on in their careers by her influence and was always most interested in all their doings. Sir Lowry, whose sister Henrietta was married to Mrs. Robinson's nephew, Lord Grantham, first met his future wife at Durnford.

Miniatures are often disappointing as portraits. But that of Mrs. Robinson is very characteristic, with lively brown eyes, rather a pointed face, a straight nose with a slight upward tilt suggesting a love of investigation. Several of the most interesting letters here were preserved by her. But her handwriting is infamous.

Here is a letter from Frances Harris to her sister Catherine—at home with her parents at Henley:

PRIVY GARDENS
11*th June*, 1814

"I wrote you a few lines by the coach this morning, my dearest Catherine, which I hope you received with the soles, etc.

I think my aunt was not exactly pleased at my being introduced to Blücher and I saw this so clearly that when I saw Hardenberg[1] at Lady Grantham's the next night, I made Frederick[2] introduce me to him and I desired him to do the same

---

[1] Prince von Hardenberg, Chancellor of Prussia, one of the signatories to the Peace of Paris.
[2] Her cousin Frederick Robinson.

to my Aunt to avoid giving her offence. I certainly was much gratified at seeing Blücher thus satisfactorily, and should have been more so had you been here to do so too! But really as to the rest of the illustrious strangers—as they are called—I do not feel a bit more that I have seen them than if they had remained at Petersburg. I cannot even pretend to have seen the King of Prussia, and as to the Emperor [of Russia] I can say I have seen the carriage in which he was and that is all. The truth is that being in London is of no use unless you are asked to the places where these great people show themselves, and they purposely conceal the hours at which they go out to avoid a crowd collecting round them—it is equally useless to run about the streets after them.

As far as I can collect the truth from Count Michel Woronzow[1] or any of the Russians, the Emperor will go to Oxford on Sunday. I will also try to find out what time he sets out. Not, I should say, early, as in that respect he is like his sister.

There seemed some idea, as my Aunt says, of Lord Pembroke's calling at Park Place[2] with Count Michel on Monday, for they are going to meet the Emperor at Oxford. Of this you will probably hear more from my Aunt or Lord Pembroke himself. Count Michel [Woronzow] is certainly a particularly agreeable person and would do well to fall in love with, but I do not feel myself in much danger. Several people have reckoned him both

---

[1] He commanded the Russian army of occupation after Waterloo. His sister was Lady Pembroke.

[2] Lord Malmesbury's house at Henley—half-way to Oxford.

THE PEACE OF PARIS

like you and Alfred. I can see it a little, though, to say the truth, notwithstanding he has a very pleasant and good countenance, I think it no compliment to either of you.

After all, I did walk about last night to see the illuminations with Frederick and was much pleased with some of them that were sufficiently sheltered to escape from being half blown out, which was the case from the high east wind with those in the public offices in Whitehall. The streets were very full and in parts crowded, but there saw very little exultation. Altogether, they say, both the illuminations themselves and the expressions of pleasure were far inferior to those after the battle of Vittoria, or for the Restoration of the Bourbons. The only shouting or applause I heard was for a cart carrying about a flag on which was written, 'We have cut down the Corn Bill'. The devices were in general merely 'Peace Unanimity' or words of such import. The Admiralty, which was altogether one of the best, had 'A Glorious War Terminating in an Honourable Peace'. As we walked down Piccadilly, the Emperor and the Grand Duchess returned from Ascot at half-past twelve o'clock and were very much cheered. . . ."

What follows may be introduced by this entry from the *General Register* for April 20th:

"On this day, Louis XVIII from his retreat at Hartwell, being summoned to assume the crown of his native kingdom, was invited by the Prince Regent first to display the royal dignity in the capital of England."

"Hon. Mrs. Robinson to the Countess of Malmesbury:

PRIVY GARDENS
April 21st, 1814

MY DEAR HARRIET,

I send you a fleur-de-lys in commemoration of your old friend's[1] entry into London yesterday! I am not able, I fear, to describe it so well as Frederick did Monsieur's entrance into Paris. Neither can it be so interesting. Yet it is a more extraordinary event to see a King of France conducted by the Regent of England into its capital in full pomp and state, drawn by the King's eight cream-coloured horses and attended by five other coaches and six, a guard of horse preceding and a numerous body of yeomanry following, besides hundreds of gentlemen on horseback making part of the procession.

The scene of Piccadilly was beautiful. It was lined by the Life Guards from Albemarle Street to Hyde Park Corner. They kept a clear passage wide enough for two carriages and behind them were rows of carriages filled with ladies, and every other space occupied by foot passengers as well as the whole of the Green Park within sight of Piccadilly! We were at the Pulteney Hotel in the very centre of everything. Our coach was immediately under the windows. The Duchess of Oldenburg, Princess Charlotte and Princesses Elizabeth and Mary[2] were on the balcony over the door, all the Russians on the circular balcony. I saw the room above—

---

[1] Louis XVIII. Lady Malmesbury, who had many friends belonging to the *ancien régime,* saw much of Louis XVIII during his exile in England.

[2] George III's daughters. They were the guests of the Duchess.

THE PEACE OF PARIS

occupied by the Duchess of Leeds, Lady Osborne, the Fagels,[1] Grantham and Fanny Temple and Harriet.

The procession appeared at half-past five and the sight was really magnificent in its way and moved very slowly. Indeed I believe the cream colours never had so long a march before, nor had the Regent ever sat back in a coach,[2] but I hope neither H.R.H. nor the horses will suffer. The band played 'Vive Henri IV' as the King passed the Pulteney Hotel and there was some cheering, but not much. In fact, the people were so eager to see that they did not give themselves time to cheer. The Russians were all astonishment at the immense population of London, and it was indeed a wonderful sight—most of them with white cockades and all in good humour. Neither did I hear of any accident whatever. People were up in the trees in the Park like so many rooks and the lamp-lighter's ladder was in requisition to mount the rails, lamp-posts and walls. The Princesses and most of the ladies wore a fleur-de-lys like that I sent you and *all* the white cockade. All the servants wore the white cockade. And it looked like a universal marriage in London!

The Duchesse d'Angoulême[3] was on the side nearest us. She looked out and smiled, but appeared very pale. The Prince [of Wales] I could not see nor

[1] Baron Fagel, Secretary of State, followed the Prince of Orange into exile when the French conquered Holland. He returned with the Prince in 1813, and in 1814 came to London as Minister Plenipotentiary to sign an alliance.

[2] He sat facing the King, presumably because both these royal personages were of such dimensions that they could not sit side by side in the coach.

[3] "Madame Royale", daughter of Louis XVI.

the King, but the former, I'm told, looked in high spirits and seemed much pleased. Puységur[1] was in one of the carriages, Monsieur Dillon[2] in another, also some ladies. Madame Moreau[3] was with the Princesses, also Madame de Lieven.[4] The little boy was there, a fine, fat, fair child. We were within sight and Princess Elizabeth discovered us and bowed. Princess Charlotte looked very pale and she had a footstool to keep her leg up. The Duchess of Leeds said she was but poorly.

The invitation card to Carlton House this morning is quite an historical document as it is worded 'To meet the Queen and the King of France'. I should have liked to have seen this assembly. . . .

It was a dry, calm day, but we wanted sun to have lighted up the scene."

On June 8th the Emperor Alexander of Russia and the King of Prussia came to England on a visit of ceremony.

"Lady Hertford to Lady Malmesbury.

DEAR LADY MALMESBURY, *June* 1814

The moment I got your letter I despatched invitation to my ball to Lady Frances Harris and Mrs. Robinson. I did not know the former was in town or I should have sent it sooner. She will tell

[1] There were six royal carriages before the State carriage. Puységur, Comte de Chastenet, was an *émigré*, one of three brothers, great believers in magnetic healing.

[2] Edward, Count Dillon, an *émigré*, one of a distinguished Irish family settled in France, all actively Royalist.

[3] Widow of the famous General who transferred his allegiance from Bonaparte to the Allies.

[4] Wife of the Russian Ambassador.

THE PEACE OF PARIS

you all about my ball and how she liked the Emperor, who was in extreme good-humour and good manners—for him. But as for presenting anyone as you desired me to, it is out of the question. That must be done by his ambassador. He talks a little, dances a vast deal, never sits down, not even to supper, and all the time he waltzes he has an air *occupé*, as if he was thinking of something else. He has not *les manières* of some friends, nor is he a beauty, but he is an extremely well-looking Sergeant! I fancy he is not very wise, and that after he has flourished a few phrases about *la libéralité, la tolérance*, etc., he cannot get a bit further. Madame de Staël said the Grand Duchess '*n'était qu'une poupée apprise*', and I have some suspicion the Emperor is much the same.

As for Blücher, I am very fond of him. Moreover, he is very fond of me. He was very drunk and amongst many tendernesses he assured me '*que j'étais une femme délicieuse, et qu'il avait le cœur fendu*'. You know his language is nearly unintelligible.

I am very sorry to say that I have not the slightest hopes of procuring a ticket for White's as each subscriber has so few and they all have been promised for ages—not even the Royal Family have any to give away. In fact, people are quite in despair and I know members who have not and cannot get tickets. My sisters and their children are in this melancholy situation and I hear nothing but weeping and wailing and gnashing of teeth.

I am tired to death of these illustrious personages and sincerely hope they will all be gone on Tuesday or Wednesday at latest.

Adieu, dear Lady Malmesbury, and believe me
Ever yours affec^{ately},
J. A. HERTFORD"

The ball is described by Mrs. Robinson to Lady Malmesbury.

"MY DEAR HARRIET, PRIVY GARDENS
June 16*th*, 1814

I think it is your turn to be written to, and especially to receive some account of Lady Hertford's ball, which was magnificent and well-managed. She was extremely civil and by her reception very much reconciled me to being, as I felt I was there, a forced invitation. It is a thing to submit to on such an occasion, but not to repeat. We also stayed to supper by Lady H.'s express invitation to me—she quite insisted on it—and indeed there was room for thirty or forty more people. The Potentates, having dined at Lord Castlereagh's and gone from hence to Covent Garden and then to the Opera, did not arrive at Lady Hertford's till near one o'clock. The Regent was the first to appear, and I think looks ill. Indeed, Sir William Farquhar advised his not going to Oxford, for he is fagged and fatigued and cannot bear the early rising. The second room on the right hand was destined to waltzing and the library for country dances. The Prince of Orange began the waltz with Lady E. Leveson, then the Emperor with Miss [*illegible*], and as I was looking on I next descried Fanny[1] waltzing with the Prince of Orange.

There were so many new and foreign faces and uniforms that I could hardly believe myself in an

---
[1] Later, Lowry Cole's wife.

English assembly. No introductions, Lady Hertford told us, could be made to the Emperor except by Mme. de Lieven, and I believe she went away before he arrived. I observed that the Prince of Orange introduced the Duchess of Wellington both to the Emperor and to the King of Prussia and these were the only exceptions. The Duke of Orleans arrived and was embraced twice by the Regent. It was quite a tender scene. The Emperor spoke to those people he knew. His mouth and his smile very much reminded me of the Empress Catherine—also his profile. There is a print very like him that Fanny shall get. He waltzes well, but his country dancing is but moderate.

We supped at three o'clock and in the largest room was the table for the Potentates, all served on gold plate. The Prince, Lady Hertford and Blücher were at one end, the Emperor at the other. The King of Prussia did not sit down to supper. There were, I guess, about sixty people at this table, and chosen according to rank.

I supped in the round room, Fanny in another, for we were divided, half in one room and half in the other. I was introduced to Count Rasonmowsky. Czernicheff[1] is a handsome and a good dancer, ditto the King of Prussia's brother[2] and Prince Augustus. There was a Prince of Mecklenburg, a good figure but the Strelitz face. The King of Prussia is well-looking but with a melancholy expression as if all this show and gaiety was irksome to him.

Fanny stayed on to please me after supper, for the dancing was then less crowded and I wished to see

---

[1] The Russian General.
[2] Prince William Augustus was the King's cousin.

these people more at my ease. The Emperor danced one country dance with Lady Grantham and two after supper with Mrs. Arbuthnot.[1] A Battu [?] was talked of, but the sett was long and I tore myself away at half-past four, leaving Alexander still dancing, and the Regent there, not willing to quit the field first!"

More detail of the time is in a letter from Capt. W. Bowles, just back from a long cruise.

H.M. *Ceres, June* 15*th*, 1814
In a thick fog near the Isle of Wight

"My dear Mrs. Robinson,
While I am waiting here till it clears up sufficiently to find my way into Spithead, I am getting my letters ready to save the post if possible, and amongst others I will prepare this bulletin of my arrival which the name of the ship would have given you no idea of. And it is necessary to explain that finding her a much better sort of command than the *Aquilon* and better able to fight Americans, I exchanged at Rio de Janeiro, taking with me my officers and men.

The glorious and almost incredible intelligence which I have been picking up by degrees on my passage makes me suspect that fighting is almost over for the present, and although I should have died happy after taking even one American I'm afraid they will be frightened into terms before I can be ready for sea again.

A pilot boat last night told me that the Emperor

[1] She and her husband lived on terms of great intimacy with the Duke of Wellington.

THE PEACE OF PARIS

of Russia, etc., etc., were to be present at a grand naval review at Portsmouth next week, so I am just in time to see some part of these most extraordinary events.

Believe me, in great haste,
Ever most affec^{ately} yours,
WILLIAM BOWLES"

The same to the same.

PORTSMOUTH
June 26*th*, 1814

"The bustle and madness of last week have completely prevented my thanking you sooner for your letter of the 16th and for your kind offer of lodgings in Privy Gardens. It is still, however, entirely uncertain what may be the final destination of the *Ceres*, and till that is arranged I must wait here for orders.

The spectacle here has really been extremely fine. The weather, though cold, has been very favourable for naval evolution and we have, I hope, not acquitted ourselves badly. No newspaper account that I have seen does justice at all to the magnificence of the review on Thursday, of which Lord Grantham and Fitzharris [her nephew, Lord Fitzharris] have probably given you full accounts already. . . .

The Regent looks rather fagged with such continued entertainments and rejoicings. The Emperor of Russia not the least altered since I saw him at St. Petersburg. Poor Blücher has been almost eaten up by the ladies here and certainly will defend them from all those imputations of prudery and reserve under which they have heretofore laboured. . . ."

CHAPTER IX

THE HUNDRED DAYS

AFTER the rejoicings and the Peace were over, Europe settled down into a false security. International affairs were being arranged by the men of renown, emperors, kings and diplomatists, assembled at Vienna. In England, we are told, there was less interest shown in the squabbles over the rectification of boundaries or the restoration of stolen portions of kingdoms, than over obtaining from such Powers as France and Spain a mandate for the abolition of the slave trade. Otherwise the reaction had set in and things were dull. Except for the war in North America, whither some of the best regiments had been sent from Spain, there was little to be anxious about.

The deliberations of the Congress might have lasted a good deal longer had not Napoleon's escape from Elba burst among them like a bombshell. He had landed in the Gulf of St. Juan near Cannes on March 1st. How this news affected other less important persons these letters will show.

"George Bowles to Hon. Mrs. Robinson.
BRUSSELS
March 12th, 1815

I am perfectly ashamed to reflect how long a time has elapsed since your last kind letter. You will not, however, impute my silence to ingratitude

THE HUNDRED DAYS

but to my wish to spare you a dull and uninteresting prose. Now, however, that Buonaparte has again made his appearance on the stage, a letter from *any* part of the Continent may perhaps not be unacceptable, however far removed from the scene of action. You must, of course, receive so much quicker intelligence via Calais than I can give you that it is almost superfluous repeating any reports now afloat here. The latest accounts we have, the Prince [of Orange] read us at dinner to-day from your old friend, General Fagel. He represents Paris as extremely tranquil and seems to have no idea of this being anything more than the last throw of a desperate gamester who sells his shirt in the hopes of winning back his fortune! His only hope of assistance must be from Murat, whose situation is nearly as desperate as his own. All things considered, it is probably the very best thing that could have happened and we shall now get rid of both at the same time! If they were to have a little success at first, it would not be amiss and would enable one to discover real friends from false ones.

This business will, I imagine, rather serve to prolong our stay in this country, as certainly the annexation of Belgium to Holland is not even yet much relished, and while Napoleon is afloat it would hardly be prudent to leave Flanders without some troops to be depended on.

The new King[1] is expected here this week with all his court for some considerable time. He is so very quiet a personage that his residence will probably not make any difference in the gaiety of

[1] Louis XVIII fled at once to Belgium on Napoleon's approach to Paris.

Brussels. The hereditary Prince [of Orange] is certainly becoming extremely popular with all the natives and most deservedly so. It is quite impossible to take more pains to please or to show greater attention to all parties than he does.

We have all been abusing London police most furiously for these last three or four days. It is really a most disgraceful circumstance to England that such performances as those which have taken place lately in the window-breaking line should be suffered with so much coolness. Our *Riot Act* stands in need of repair quite as much as, I fear, Robinson's house[1] in Burlington Gardens must do. I trust, however, there is no chance of his or any other promoter of the Corn Bill being bullied out of what is so absolutely necessary for the good of the country. . . .

The news from America is really too bad to think of. I could find it in my heart to write a complete Jeremiade on such a termination to such a war. . . ."

"Countess of Pembroke to the Hon. Mrs. Robinson.

WINDSOR CASTLE
MY DEAR MRS. ROBINSON, *Monday, March 27th,* 1815

I am seized with an earnest desire to know what you and your circle of friends are feeling and thinking of all these horrid events, or rather this one event that seems for the moment to swallow up all the others. The celerity of it all surprises me, and to find by it that no care was taken to watch the

---

[1] Robinson as Vice-President of the Board of Trade introduced on March 1st a bill forbidding imports of wheat till the English price should be 80s. a quarter. Riots followed on March 6th and Robinson's house, as well as those of other leading supporters of the Bill, was wrecked by the mob.

movements of that man after placing him on that island! I never doubted but that he would begin his machinations as soon as the Congress was over, but there was no imagining that no precautions were taken for watching him, enough to have a fleet out immediately to stop his landing! It was bad enough to let him go there and call him Emperor. But now, having declared him an outlaw, there will be no more temporising with him and I hope the Allies are advancing their troops quick.

Think of poor Lady Fitzroy Somerset obliged to lie in at Paris! What a set of people the French are! It seems as if formerly their enthusiasm for their Royal Family had been the only principle that actuated them and had produced even many fine actions, and that, *that* annihilated, they had none left! It is all apathy! The civil part only caring to amuse themselves, the military to fight and plunder, which they think themselves sure of with Bony!

What says Lord Malmesbury?

I still have a hope that Bony's end will be being caught by a party of Cossacks and then I would let them put a stone round his neck and drown him as a venomous animal. No nobler death than that!

I remain here till Friday next, and shall be in London by dinner that day. And on the Tuesday after shall go to Brighton for a week. It would be pretty of you if you would call in on Friday evening between the hours of seven and ten, if you can spare an hour or even half-an-hour, and we will give you some tea—that is all I can promise you.

I am,
Ever yours sincerely, dear Mrs. Robinson,
ELIZABETH PEMBROKE"

These were the sentiments of a Russian, not an Englishwoman. Lady Pembroke was sister to Count Woronzow.

Meantime Lowry Cole, though still on duty as Lieut.-General (he had been promoted in 1813 and was holding the Northern Command), felt unhappy about his position, and discontented because his services had received no considerable recognition. Opinion in general regarded him and Sir Thomas Picton as great soldiers who had been shabbily treated. He also thought rewards due; but what he wanted now was a fresh opportunity to distinguish himself, as appears by this letter to Lady Grantham, dated March 29th, 1815:

"I have been every day in the last fortnight intending to write to you, but have been so unhinged, what with the loss of my poor friend, Edward Pakenham,[1] and the sad prospect which the return of Bonaparte to power offers to Europe, that I have really not been able to write even to you, my love. When the misery of so many millions of people is concerned, it is the acme of selfishness to think of oneself, and yet self will intrude on mine in spite of myself.

"I have been in doubt whether to offer my services in case of a war, which I believe to be inevitable, and have pretty nearly determined not to offer them. If they are wanted, they may ask for them. This compliment at least, I think, I have a right to expect from the Government!

"Every feeling in me of honourable ambition is

[1] Killed in the American War.

crushed by what I feel unmerited neglect. It is foolish, I believe, to give way to these feelings, but they get the better of me in spite of myself. Had I the means of retiring from public life, I would not hesitate in doing so—and with what I have, were it not for my friends, would do so. I have written for leave to go to town to take my seat. As I presume it will not be refused, I propose going there next week."

While affairs were in this position, Cole received a letter from Captain Henry Dumaresq, who had been his A.D.C. during the Peninsular War and was now on General Byng's staff. The letter throws a pleasant light on Cole's relations with his subordinates in the Fourth Division.

COLCHESTER
"MY DEAR SIR LOWRY,   *April 2nd,* 1815
What do you think of affairs, Sir? And will there be an opportunity of we young chaps enlisting again under the Beau,[1] do you imagine? . . .
Pray where is Wade?[2] and what has he done to get away from France? I conclude you will now soon have him at York, as it would not be safe for him as a *militaire* to remain under the government of Monsieur l'Empereur!
'*Qui viva que nina Napoleon*', we may surely say, for he has at any rate kept second battalions (some at least) alive, and whether immediately or not gives us reason to hope for a long and bloody war!
The moment Lady Byng is brought to bed—

[1] A nickname for the Duke of Wellington.
[2] Sir Lowry's divisional staff officer in the Peninsula.

which I should have been two months ago had I been half as large as she is—the General intends going up to town and finding out from the heads what are the intentions of our ministers in regard to sending troops to the Netherlands. I told you, I think, he purposed being of the party, if they would employ him, and has offered his services. Should he not be sent out immediately, he has been good enough to promise me his best interests in getting me there, which the moment I heard of any force being employed I candidly told him was my wish; being convinced as I am it's so much my interest to do so. Although it's impossible to be more comfortable than I am here, *Gracias a Dios*, I am not yet arrived at an age when enjoyments are to be allowed to stand in the way of probable advancement, and though persuaded he will be ultimately employed when the troops perhaps return from the coast of America and from Canada, should the intention of the Allies be to reinstate the Bourbons, I should wish to be as early in the field as possible.

It's impossible to evince more kindness than Tiger [General Byng] has, and when I gave him a sort of warning, he was good enough to say he thought I should do perfectly right in going out, and would further my wishes by his interest, and he recommends my remaining quiet for some time.

May I ask your advice, my dear Sir Lowry, as to the policy of timid backwardness and amiable tranquillity? I feel great vanity and no small pleasure in telling you the Duke has recommended me for the Brevet, through the kind means, I know, of Fitzroy,[1] which, whether attended or no with

[1] Lord Fitzroy Somerset, the Duke's Military Secretary.

immediate promotion, is at any rate a flattering instance of his opinion and a most pleasing assurance of Fitzroy's sincerity. . . .

This time last year we were in the white house near Calommiers! To-morrow night, the delightful march we had towards Grenada! I still continue to think and fear those were the happiest moments of my life! However, I will always make the best of it!

And most sincerely wishing you every good wish you can desire,

Believe me, my dear Sir Lowry,

Ever your most sincerely and gratefully attached

A. Dumaresq"

Shortly after this, Cole received from the Duke a summons to reassume command of the 4th Division. But in the meantime he had at last brought matters to a head with Lady Frances Harris, and, determined to be employed, was no less determined to be married. Yet it is an amazing proof how inadequately the military situation was realised that sixteen days before Waterloo was fought he should have asked for leave of absence, and should have got it. Here is his letter to Lord Fitzroy Somerset, dated London, May 30th, 1815:

"My dear Fitzroy,

Having determined within these few days on following your example by becoming a Benedict, it is my wish as well as that of my intended, Lady Frances Harris, to have the ceremony over if possible previous to my starting for your Army.

At the same time, as I should on no account wish and should feel much annoyed to be absent in case of active operations taking place, I write this to request you will mention my situation to the Duke and if it is not an improper request ask him if under these circumstances he thinks I might prolong my stay in town for three weeks from hence.

I should add that under no circumstances is it my intention that the lady should accompany me, and I should send off my baggage and horses and A.D.C. and in the course of this week to be ready to start at a moment's notice. As I shall be impatient for answer, pray give me a line at the very first opportunity.

Believe me to remain, etc.,
G. Lowry Cole"

This request was granted.

There was no time for delay, scarcely even for those arrangements considered in those days most necessary, marriage settlements. Lord Malmesbury did all in his power to smooth over the difficulty. Miss Cozens was one of the first to hear of her engagement from Lady Frances Harris, who wrote to her:

Richmond House
May 27th, 1815

"Tho' I believe Catherine [her sister] has been writing to you very fully, my dearest Co., I could not let anybody but myself communicate to you any event so interesting to myself as that which will result from all that has passed since yesterday. It will not, I daresay, be a matter of surprise to you to hear that Sir Lowry Cole has proposed to me and perhaps as little so that I have accepted him, for Cath has, I believe, kept you *au fait*.

You may imagine what an inexpressible comfort it is to me to find my choice approved by my Father and all those belonging to me here, and I don't fear, my dearest Co., *your* objecting when you know this to be the case, and still less when you see him for whom I bespeak the promise at least of the warm affection you have always borne to me. The thing was only settled this morning. . . . I am not of an age or a disposition to take such a step without fear and trembling. But where I am secure of a good heart and good principles, religious and moral, I know not why I should not do so.

My Father has been all kindness and compliance, Catherine of course the former with less of the latter.
Yours most affec^{ately},
F. H."

Nothing about her mother's feelings. There are, however, a few sidelights on the subject in some of the letters of congratulation. This one is dated "Minto", and must be from her aunt, Lady Minto, or one of her cousins there.

"Anne is like all your friends in hopes that you will be Sir Lowry's wife before he sails. . . . Lady Malmesbury is growing as fond of him as you could wish. Although I believe before she had made more acquaintance with Sir Lowry, she had too strong a prepossession in favour of an older and less brilliant admirer of yours not to wish you to make another choice. I wish Catherine would console the interesting widower. I believe him to be very excellent, but in comparison with Sir Lowry he is what Mrs.

Bethune would call 'a docken to a tansy'. Lady Malmesbury talks very amiably of her pleasure in the expression of happiness on your face and of the comfort she expects from Sir Lowry's open and affectionate disposition."

One of her cousins, Anne Elliot, expressing her joy at the news, writes:

"I am not in the slightest degree acquainted with Sir Lowry, but all I have ever heard of him satisfies me that your choice is an excellent one and I am quite glad that I have been often enough in company with him to remember at least his appearance, for I should be sorry you should be married to a man whom I did not know even by sight!

"I remember in 1805 seeing Sir Lowry at Mrs. Robinson's and hearing that he admired you. He is a pattern of constancy worthy of the days of Amadis if he has carried his love for you about with him all this time. At all events it is pleasant *à notre âge* that one's husband should be an old acquaintance. At least I feel myself the complete impossibility of marrying a new one! And as during the whole of that long acquaintance you never can have heard anything but good of him, you marry upon sure ground without any of the usual risks of matrimony.

"My prayer is that you may be his wife before you part; your situation otherwise will be a most unpleasant one. Anxiety and uneasiness you must have, and so long as a woman is not married she is not permitted to speak openly of her feelings. Besides, if Sir Lowry was unwell and you could not go to him you would be doubly uncomfortable. Tho' perhaps he might object to your coming to him at the Army, he *might* be so situated as for you to be with him in comfort and safety. In short, I think, and all your friends think, you *ought* to marry before he leaves you! . . . I wish, and from what Lady Malmesbury says, I hope you and Sir Lowry will be convinced of this and marry even if you should part at the church door!"

Captain William Bowles, a close friend of the family, wrote to Miss Harris, aunt of Lady Frances:

2nd June, 1815
"MY DEAR MRS. HARRIS,
　　I have rather delayed writing to you, not, you may be sure, from the want of a most sincere and cordial participation in the satisfaction you will have felt, but because I hoped that after having seen Sir Lowry Cole a little I might be able to send you something more satisfactory than a common letter of congratulation could have contained four days ago! And I know you will be pleased to read another confirmation of the praises which have already been sent you of him.
　　I need not tell you that there are few officers of his age and standing who have seen so much service in such various climates or who have distinguished themselves so much. But his manners in private life betray no consciousness of his own merits and are mild and unassuming, tho' lively and animated, and his conversation full of information. I am sure that you will like him and flatter myself that my additional testimony will add some weight to those

of your less unprejudiced though scarcely less interested correspondents.

There are of course some drawbacks and some circumstances to regret, but they are only such as are incidental to all connexions formed with military men, and *your* friend Buonaparte has, luckily for us, made us such necessary (I do not say valuable) members of society that you will be inclined to make due allowance for the inconvenience we sometimes occasion.

And there being, as we long ago agreed, no such thing as perfect happiness, let us hope the choice Lady Frances has made will produce for her as large a proportion as can be reasonably expected.

We are all now on the tiptoe of expectation as to the events which the next fortnight will produce. Important they must be beyond all former precedent, but I am very sanguine in my expectations of beating Buonaparte again for the third time.

Are you not tired of such a long prose?

Your most affec^{ate} and faithful
WILLIAM BOWLES"

LONDON
June 2nd, 1815

The next letter is from her sister on the wedding day:

15*th June,* 1815

"MY DEAREST FANNY,

I think you will like to have a line from me to tell you that my Father seems in no respect the worse for his exertions this morning—that he found the Church neither hot nor cold and that he seems perfectly well and very composedly happy.

I am quite sure that no event in the world could

have made him nearly so much so, which must be an inexpressible addition to your happiness. As for me, it seems like a dream that my daily prayer for you should be now accomplished and that you are actually *that* I have so ardently hoped one day to see you. For you know it has always been *my* decided opinion, and though you and I have sometimes differed on it (we never shall again, I think) that real happiness is only to be found in those near and dear ties which bind you to one, thank God, I feel so sure is deserving of you in every way. And I assure you he has a large share in my feelings of gratitude to-day, for perhaps he is the only man, certainly the only one I know, who has contrived to inspire me with such complete confidence in his kind and excellent heart and principles that he has robbed me of all nervousness for your future comfort and happiness so far as it is in his power!"

Lowry Cole, on his part, wrote to his sister Lady Florence Balfour:

LONDON
June 6th, 1815

"A thousand thanks for your very affectionate letter without a date! But more especially for that which you wrote Fanny, which has gratified her very much.

I have no fear of your not loving her the more you know her, and I do hope that you who hitherto have always been dearest in affection to my heart may be equally so to her. All her family are as kind to me as possible, and Lord Malmesbury, to facilitate our being married before I start, proposed of his own accord to take my Bond for the £10,000 and that we should be married. She is to remain with him during my absence from her own desire as well as his."

Although what seemed almost indecent haste was used over the important business of marriage settlements between members of two great landed families, the upshot was that June 15th, 1815, found Lowry Cole a married man in London, and the Fourth Division under another commander. Lady Frances Cole wept bitterly when the news of the victory came in, lest she should have caused disappointment to her soldier. But tears must have exchanged for a natural relief when she learnt that Sir Thomas Picton, who commanded in Cole's place, fell on the field.

SIR GALBRAITH LOWRY COLE
second son of the first Earl of Enniskillen

[From the picture by Lawrence

LADY FRANCES HARRIS
second daughter of the first Earl of Malmesbury
Married, 1815, Sir G. Lowry Cole

CHAPTER X

AFTER WATERLOO

A FORTNIGHT after his marriage Sir Lowry departed for Flanders with a faint hope that there might still be laurels to be gathered. It was hard to part from his wife no doubt, and the following letters to my grandmother show how mixed were his feelings. They also give an interesting description of the days after Waterloo. He was accompanied by his brother-in-law, Lord Grantham.

"To Lady Frances Cole.

RAMSGATE
June 29th, 1815

MY DEAREST FANNY,

Having a few hours' leisure as we are not to embark before 2 o'clock P.M., I cannot—at least in my own opinion, let you think what you please—employ a part of the time better than in repeating what I have so very often told you in this last fortnight, that you are dearer to my heart than I can say.

I am annoyed at this delay, for, having once parted from you, I am anxious to get to the army as soon as possible, altho' the Field for Honor and Glory is, I believe and hope for the sake of my country, now at an end.

However I may regret—for I cannot help feeling a sort of regret at not having witnessed the glorious result of Waterloo—I feel at the same time that it is by no means improbable that I might not have survived that day! This thought consoles me as I should be sorry *now* to quit this world, however indifferent—at least with respect to my own feelings—I might have been previous to knowing you.

God bless you, my love, and preserve you to me. I wish I had told you to write me a line yesterday evening. Being silly enough to think you might have done so, I went to the Post Office and was so unreasonable as to be disappointed at not finding a letter! . . .

God bless you, my Heart, and believe me to be devotedly and affectionately your own

G. L. C."

OSTEND
Friday, 30th June

"MY DEAREST FANNY,

We are just arrived after a passage of twenty hours with the wind direct against us. And as you are and always will be uppermost in my thoughts in future, I hasten to comply with your orders—or wishes.

The only news that I have is that the Austrians and Bavarians are advancing rapidly, and that it is said that the Duke has halted at Laon to let them come up, probably not wishing to risk anything.

The wounded in general are doing well. Lord Uxbridge, F. Somerset and the Prince of Orange are walking out. This Lord Rendlesham told me. Colonel Delancy is, I am sorry to say, dead.

God bless and take care of you. Possibly you may not hear from me for some time, as having quitted *you*, I must now attend to my Mistress Bellona and shall lose no time in joining the Duke.

AFTER WATERLOO

We start in an hour for Brussels, accompanied by my Lord Grantham."

To the same.

BRUSSELS
Saturday

"We arrived here, having travelled all night, and are to start to-morrow for the Army. I have been really quite melancholy since I came at seeing all my mangled friends, and to confess the truth am not divested of a feeling that I ought to have shared the danger with them, but am inclined to feel at the same time that all is for the best. For, had I been there, I might not perhaps have been at this moment alive and bless'd with one of the first of her sex as a wife! You see, my Heart, I am not afraid to open my inmost feelings to you! . . .

G. LOWRY COLE"

Here may be set in "little Aunt Robinson's" first-hand account of the field of Waterloo, as it was three weeks after the battle. She wrote:

Thursday, July 20th, 1815

"Lord Grantham called on me. He was just returned from a most curious and interesting tour of nearly three weeks, having gone over with Sir Lowry Cole who left England on the 29th June to join the Army. They passed over the ground where the famous and ever memorable Battle of Waterloo had been fought. It is a small space and without any sort of natural or artificial defence whatever. It was then so completely cleared of the dead, who had been buried or burnt, that nothing disgusting or unpleasant was to be seen. They joined the Duke of Wellington at Brussels (I *think*) and he entered into the most curious and interesting details of the Battle of Waterloo, which he said had been lost and won more than once. The Duke alone may be said to have accomplished the final victory as he would persist in pursuing the enemy against the opinion of many of his generals, Lord Uxbridge amongst others, who said it was better to rest satisfied with the advantages they had and what had been done. The Duke said, 'I am responsible and I'll do it!' and it succeeded. The Prussians arrived most opportunely, and when they met the British troops their bands struck up 'God save the King'.

Lord Grantham entered Paris with the Duke of Wellington, who did not go in, as had once been intended, at the head of his army but merely with his aides-de-camp, the Duke in his plain blue coat mounted on a favourite grey horse, the others all in their uniforms. The curiosity of the Parisians to see them was very great and when Lord Grantham, Sir Lowry and the A.D.C. went to some shops in the Palais Royal in order to buy something as a memorial of the day of this extraordinary entrance into Paris, the people followed them in crowds. Many were disposed to be insolent, to hitch in their spurs and try to pick a quarrel, and Lord Grantham said he was several times afraid Sir Lowry's Irish blood would have made him angry! In general they are disposed to favour the English and say, *Les Anglais sont doux comme des demoiselles.*

An *English* guard of honour received the Emperor of Austria and the King of Prussia. How strange the English doing the honours of Paris!!! The Duke

AFTER WATERLOO

of Wellington gave his great dinner to the generals, etc., in a low room at Verrey's, the most celebrated Restaurateur.

The dinner well dressed; I suppose it was at this dinner that Blücher gave the toast Bowles mentions in a letter from Paris on the 10th July. When most of the usual toasts had been drunk, Blücher desired to give this one, 'May the Ministers and Ambassadors not spoil what the armies have so gloriously begun'.

Lord Grantham, previous to entering Paris, had been billeted at some gentleman's villa about six miles off where he found every window broken, all the mirrors destroyed, and the furniture of every description spoiled or taken away. Cavalry bivouacking in a very pretty flower garden and on the statues of Nymph and Venus were hung the soldiers' pantaloons, etc.

Most of the villas were pillaged, but not St. Cloud or Malmaison, except of a few books, and it was from hence Sir Lowry took Florian's *Don Quixote* which he sent to Fanny.

The English Army is fed by the French, and the Generals of Divisions all quartered in the houses of private individuals. The Mayor of each quartier gives an order for the purpose, and Lord Grantham went with Sir Lowry's A.D.C.'s to choose one for him. They saw several. Sometimes the people were civil, sometimes sulky, sometimes supplicating. They ended by taking a house on the Boulevards which belonged to a General Marais, supposed to be a Bonapartist. The people in Paris were in general silent and sulky."

From Sir Lowry Cole to his wife.

          Neuilly
"My dearest Fanny,   Near Paris
  I was made more happy yesterday evening than I have been since we parted by receiving your letter of the 30th, notwithstanding the very long lecture it contains. . . .
  Whatever are my feelings in not having been present at Waterloo, I have none as to what people may say of my absence. I am confident no person could suppose I wished to avoid it. On the contrary, all who know me at all, I am equally sure, give me credit for the very reverse. The Duke, I know, does me full justice on that score! Nor have I heard, my love, or do I believe, that anyone attributes any undue influence on your part or supposes that I made any unnecessary delay in joining the Army afterwards. You need not therefore feel uncomfortable in that respect.
  Nothing can be more cordial or kind than the Duke has been to me since my arrival. He has willingly complied with any little request I have made, and even anticipated me in some I was most anxious for.
  I am but just returned from seeing his entry into Paris. The proudest day of his life and, I think I may add, that of his country. I confess I felt not a little so myself on this occasion.
  The Parisians were anything but cordial in their reception of us. Nor is it to be wondered at, as nothing can be much more mortifying to any nation, and how much more must it be to the vainest people under Heaven!
  There are still doubts whether the King will be

reinstated or not. With the leading people here he is not popular. I believe more from his being too good for them than from any just cause of dislike. Many—and with more reason, I think—object to him from the supposition that his want of energy will keep them constantly in hot water and liable to another revolution. The peasantry and country gentlemen, so far as I can judge, appear generally in his favour.

Lord Castlereagh has arrived and a few days will probably decide the question whether he is to be reinstated or not. Fouché, report says, is in his favour. He and Talleyrand met in this house a few nights ago and talked over the business till three o'clock in the morning.

The French Army has retired beyond the Loire, commanded by Davoust. They are extremely insolent and mortified. Carnot is said to be with them, but it is not known where Bonaparte is. Some say he is gone to Cherbourg and some to Rochefort.

I am at present in command of the Reserve, consisting of the 5th and 6th Divisions and the Duke of Brunswick's Corps. And as it is possible that no one senior to me will come out under existing circumstances, I may retain the command. If we are not obliged to follow the French Army, it is of no consequence, but if we are obliged to do so I should of course wish to keep it. The Duke asked me this morning if you intended joining me here, which I of course said I wished, if all was quiet and hostilities ceased. He said that a few days would probably determine the question.

The Emperors and Kings are expected in a few

days as I am told. Grantham seems pleased with his trip. George Elliot and Bowles have arrived and are to dine with me this day, but if I had Fortunatus' cap, I would cut them and dine with you!"

Next day, he could make plans. The letter, like others concerning her comfort, has a trace of the man used to drafting operation orders.

"My dearest Fanny,
Neuilly
12th July

Having written you a longish letter yesterday, I should not have thought of writing to-day, but that Grantham talks of leaving me this evening for Calais, and as he proposes going direct from Dover to Tonbridge this letter may reach you first. Besides which, you might be disappointed at not receiving a letter from hence, and I should be sorry, my love, to give you even a momentary displeasure.

Although I know the pleasure it will give Net [Lady Grantham] to have Grantham back with her, I should not be sorry to detain him a short time longer, if his going was not likely to hasten your arrival.

What I may have left out in my letter respecting your accommodation here, he will be able to explain. I have requested him to look out in Calais and see what sort of carriages are to be hired there, as your own carriage, I presume, cannot be ready by the time you will start, and I saw nothing at Mr. Lucas' that I think will answer for a travelling carriage. If, however, you can get a comfortable one to hire on tolerably reasonable terms in London, it would be better to do so.

AFTER WATERLOO

As I hope our stay abroad will not be very long, the fewer things you bring out with you the better, as you would probably wish to buy a good many articles to bring back with you. But you will of course act in this as you like. A couple of pairs of sheets are good things to have if not absolutely necessary. And as you may wish to ride, a side-saddle will be useful. But as it would be cumbersome to carry, you may have it sent from London to Dover by the stage, on by water, and from Calais it can come by the Diligence.

If Grantham can take it, I shall send a small ornamental cup and saucer which I bought on the day the Duke entered Paris, to show you that even on that day you were not out of my thoughts. Also one or two trifling things of no value, except that when I go near a shop I am thinking if there is anything you might like. You will no doubt say this is nonsense and that I cannot afford it. But, though you may say and think so, I am sure at least it will none the less gratify you and this thought gives me too much pleasure not to indulge myself.

I have just heard that the 'Dandy Emperor' and the King of Prussia have expressed a wish to see the Army in review. The day is not fixed, but it is to be soon. Grantham will probably remain to see it. . . .

There is no news whatever—at least I have heard none. The Emperor of Austria has arrived. Everything is quiet and the people apparently satisfied with having Louis back again, although mortified at his being in a great degree forced on them. The Prussians are not very popular as they take no pains to make themselves so and plunder all the country. Their conduct compared with ours is of advantage to us!

They talk of taking away the pillar in the Place Vendôme made of the cannon taken in Germany. This I think but right, and it has been suggested that we should take the famous horses taken from Venice. I wish but I don't think we shall do so. . . .
  God bless you, my heart,
    Believe me ever,
      Your attached and affec^{ate}
        G. L. COLE

On reflection, I think you had better bring out a carriage *coûte que coûte* with you. Grantham must go to town and can see about it or write to someone. . . ."

The same to the same.

PARIS
20*th July*, 1815

"Nothing has taken place here since I wrote, except the account of Bonaparte's having surrendered to one of our ships. I have no doubt ministers are at a loss to know what to do with him. Whatever they decide on, I hope they will take care he doesn't again escape. What is to be done with the French Army is not, I believe, yet decided on—at least it has not transpired if it is so!"

NEUILLY
23*rd July*

"MY OWN DEAREST FANNY,
  I feel I am a very unreasonable being, for altho' I entirely approve of your determination to wait for the Granthams and travel with them, and that I think him perfectly right in wishing to con-

tinue drinking the waters for some time longer, I cannot help feeling, my love, not a little disappointed at the idea of not seeing you for so long a period—for it appears so to me—having buoyed myself up in the hopes of seeing you at latest the end of this week.

I have, however, another reason for wishing you not to delay longer than the date you have mentioned, as it is said that the army is to be put in cantonments and a part of it only to remain in the neighbourhood of Paris. In this case it is very probable the Corps I command may be among those which move from hence. I have no doubt I can get leave to remain in Paris some time after the move, but perhaps not so long as you might wish to remain here. Therefore on your own as well as the Granthams' account, do not stay longer in London than is necessary to fix the Grantham children. If you are at all in haste, you may with ease be here in five days, including the day you leave London. I must recommend early rising to leave in case of accidents the day before. I am told you can get good, or at least tolerable, accommodation at Boulogne, Montreuil, Abbeville and Beauvais. Abbeville is the best on the road and by setting off at daylight you may reach Paris from it in one day. You should not, however, come into town late. If I know which day you are likely to come, I could meet you part of the way."

Now follow extracts from Lady Frances Cole's diary. And here I would remark that these people who lived in most stirring times and had every opportunity of knowing the chief actors in the political drama and of hearing and seeing and understanding the inwardness of the events passing before their eyes, do not seem to have taken advantage of their exceptional opportunities. They all conscientiously kept careful diaries, in which they confided not at all. There is not an entry in either Lady Malmesbury's or Lady Frances Cole's betraying personal feeling or that might not have been shouted on the housetops; and as for Sir Lowry, he appears to have taken little interest in anything but the barometer! And yet no one of this group wrote for publication. I suppose a decent habit of reserve or reticence was too much for them, or did they lack humour—although the ladies had the character of being witty? Well, we are the losers!

In Lady Frances's diary, from which I now quote, one scarcely realises the woman happily married a few weeks before going to join her husband. She seems so calm, so unexcited. Lady Malmesbury, on the other hand, is eager for the fray, but all the same a poor diarist!

From Lady Frances Cole's diary.

August 3rd, 1815

"Left London a little before six with my mother and Fanny Temple [Lord Palmerston's sister] on my way to Paris to join Lowry—exactly the day seven weeks after I married!

"The road was new to me almost the whole way—and inferior in beauty to the Tunbridge side of the county of Kent. The approach to Dover less striking than I expected, but the Castle and Cliffs are very fine from the beach. We have been twelve hours and a half on the road in a Chaise and pair with which I came the whole way without any difficulty being made. I have people and luggage upon it.

"The Granthams joined us about nine o'clock.

August 4th

"We embarked upon the *Queen Charlotte* Packet, which we hired entirely for ourselves for thirty guineas. A delightful day and the wind perfectly favourable. We were detained till half-past eight waiting for the things to be got out of the Custom House. Captain Winthrop, who breakfasted with us, stayed on board till we sailed.

"It was impossible to have a more favourable passage. We embarked from the pier and got in one tide—about four and a half hours—to that of Calais, upon which we stepped out of the boat.

"The town of Calais consists of mean streets, narrow, and is very thinly populated in comparison to any of our maritime towns, the grass growing in many parts and the whole wearing therefore an air of solitude and desolation scarcely or ever to be met with in England.

"Intended getting on to Boulogne, but after waiting a considerable time before the carriages, etc., could be got out of the Custom House, and some time again for the arrival of the horses, we found ourselves so late that we deferred setting off till to-morrow.

"The white cockade is universally worn and the Bourgeoisie present the guard. The waiter told us they heard the cannon of the Battle of Waterloo, but were not allowed to know the result till near a fortnight after it took place. The gates of the city were ordered to be shut, the town provisioned for six months, and every preparation made for a siege. The Bourgeoisie is generally well-disposed to the Bourbons.

August 6th

"Set out from Abbeville so early that I had no time to walk about it. We found plenty of horses and got very quickly to Amiens, which is by far the handsomest town I have seen yet. The houses generally speaking and the principal building especially, of rich and handsome architecture, giving the streets a striking appearance.

"We found an excellent inn—the Hôtel des Ambassadeurs—and a room furnished quite like a drawing-room in a gentleman's house. We went immediately to see the Cathedral, which is well worth going round a *post or two* to see. . . . Some English Dragoons and a regiment of Hanoverians were quartered here and a garrison of 4,000 English is expected soon. I trust I shall not find the Army just leaving it when I reach Paris."

A few lines on the charm of the country near Paris follow, and then the climax:

"At St. Denys—the last port—Lowry met us and I had the satisfaction of hearing that this army was not yet on the move!

"We entered Paris by the Faubourg de Clichy, in itself not the best or most striking entrance, but the Bivouac of English troops, the recollections that the view of Montmartre brought to one's mind, mixed with the total change in my own situation

AFTER WATERLOO

and feelings, made me feel most strange and almost bewildered!

"I found a very handsome and comfortable Hôtel, upon which Lowry had put his *billet* and which he had taken from a General Marais. It is at the corner of the Rue Grammont on the Boulevards.

"Soon after we arrived, we walked to the Place Vendôme—the Pillar erected by Bonaparte of the German cannon. Very beautiful. I should like to see it placed in London!

"From thence to the Tuileries, with which I was greatly struck—more from the size of the Palace and gardens than from their actual beauty.

"In the evening we were too tired to do anything but write to England by the Messenger who was setting out, and go to bed early.

Wednesday, 9th August

"Went in the Duke of Wellington's carriage to see a very fine review of the Russian troops which took place in the Place Louis XV. A beautiful show but much more interesting from the ideas connected with it. We were exactly opposite the Emperors of Austria and Russia, but the sight of the Hero of Waterloo was more gratifying to an English heart! His carriage was privileged and we saw everything well. It was much stared at as we passed along and there is no doubt that he is by far the most popular of the Commanders, from the good discipline which has been observed by the whole English army.

Friday, 11th

"Rode to Neuilly with Lowry—on my new

horse. He has got the Princess Borghese's villa there —quite a palace. With a camp in the garden and park. It is occupied by the British and Hanoverians. The mixture of luxury and ornament of the villa, contrasted with the soldiers' tents and baggage, etc., made it a curious sight.

"We afterwards rode round the Bois de Boulogne where the Guards are encamped."

At this point may be added from the correspondence an intimate description of Napoleon, just as he was disappearing for ever from the scene where he had been paramount in importance and power for close upon twenty years. It was written by Sir George Bingham, who was sent out in charge of the captive. It is impartial and bears the stamp of truth and shows misfortune being borne with dignity.

H.M. Ship *Northumberland*
"My dear Sir Lowry, 1815
The orders under which I embarked for St. Helena were so sudden that I had no time to wish you an adieu previous to my leaving England. I take the opportunity of doing so now, as letters are to be forwarded from Madeira. I suppose this will find you in France and I think you will like to know how your friend Napoleon is going on.

At first he was in rather low spirits. He has now recovered and having got over the sea-sickness is very entertaining. He passes his days, in which you know on board there is no variety, in the following manner. He breakfasts in his own cabin and seldom makes his appearance before two or three o'clock. He then plays chess with some of the French who have accompanied him, who are too good courtiers ever to win a game from him. At five he comes to dinner. We sit down twelve. At table he eats voraciously and asks a number of questions. He rises almost immediately after dinner and walks the decks, talking with anyone who understands French, till eight o'clock. We then assemble in the Admiral's cabin and play Vingt-un. At ten o'clock and sometimes before he rises and goes to bed.

He has one servant who sleeps in the cabin with him and one at the door. He answers with apparent frankness any question that is asked him relative to his former transactions. He talks of Lord Wellington as being equal in the field to himself, but more fortunate in politics. He tells the same story of the battle of Waterloo that he did in his official account, namely, that the day was lost by the malevolent raising of the cry of *'Sauve qui peut'*. But he adds that 'if there had been daylight I should have remedied that, for I should have thrown aside my cloak and every Frenchman would have rallied round me'. Why he did not try that expedient the next day he did not condescend to explain. I cannot find that he used much personal exertion or even exposed himself much during the course of the day. None of his personal staff were wounded, which they could not all have escaped had he been like our Commander in the thickest part of the fight.

The Staff, like true Frenchmen, will not allow themselves to have been fairly beaten even here. They as usual tell nothing but lies, disguising numbers, etc. They cannot, however, refrain from allowing that our Infantry and Artillery are beyond praise. One of them said they were exactly what the French were before the battle of Austerlitz, since which time, according to the Comte de Montholon's account, they have never had an army, the introduction of titles having ruined it. Upon which, Madame his wife, who is on board, puts in that her husband has always been a republican.

On board Napoleon is always treated with great respect but without royal honours, except by his attendants. He continues to wear a plain green uniform with two plain epaulettes, the Star of the Legion of Honor and three small crosses in his buttonhole, white waistcoat and breeches, silk stockings and small gold buckles.

I need not describe his person to you. He has grown fat and gives me more the idea of a greasy Portuguese priest than of a person who has made so great a noise in the world. On his snuffbox he has antique coins of Sylla, Regulus, Pompey and Julius Caesar, which box Madame Bertrand says he has carried with him on most of his campaigns.

I suppose the expected ship will bring me home, for if Sir Hudson Lowe comes out it is not probable Government will allow two Major-Generals to remain in the island. Under this supposition I have left Lady Bingham at home. I wished to have escaped the voyage altogether, but was unable to do so. I should have been much more fortunate had I been with you.

The thing I feel as most uncomfortable is that I was not able to procure in London any instructions for my conduct, except from Lord Bathurst, to put myself on shore as well as on board under the orders of Sir George Cockburn, who is to be supreme and is to have the whole arrangement of the island with liberty to retain or send away the accompanying [?] troops as he chooses, to call for troops from the Cape, etc. He intends to be General as well as Admiral and has horses and furniture embarked for the purpose.

I beg to be remembered to all my old friends, and only consider myself as truly unfortunate in not having been with you and them, instead of being Napoleon's gaoler, which is a post I cannot say I ever coveted!

I remain, my dear General,
Ever sincerely yours,
G. B. BINGHAM"

CHAPTER XI

PARIS AFTER THE RESTORATION

NEITHER Sir Lowry nor his wife can have been satisfied by the circumstances of their honeymoon, which had to be spent in a crowd. Even in their home they were not alone.

On their arrival in Paris, Lord and Lady Grantham took up their residence at the Hôtel d'Abrantès on the Boulevards and went everywhere with them. Sir Lowry, being Irish, was delighted to collect his beloved family round him and to give them the best of everything. He had grasped, however, that this needed somewhat of a sacrifice on his wife's part; for in a letter from Paris previously he had thanked her "for not accepting the Granthams' offer to give up their claim to accommodation in our house"; and he tells her that though Lady Grantham is his favourite sister his wife need not be jealous of her.

But there was yet another trial in store for them both. Lady Malmesbury suddenly arranged to come to Paris.

"I am, I confess," Sir Lowry writes, "rather discomfited at Mama's determination to accompany you. I shall of course do the best I can for her accommodation."

There is no doubt that Lady Frances did not wish for her mother's company either. Lady Malmesbury was obviously a difficult woman to do with and terribly outspoken. The fact that she disliked the Duke of Wellington and repeated the abuse her French friends showered on him was very trying to her daughter; for Sir Lowry was a great admirer and friend of the Commander-in-Chief and would be ready to speak his mind also pretty plainly in his defence. It was hard to have such elements of discord introduced into her honeymoon, and I think it explains a certain depression which creeps into her letters to Miss Cozens.

Then in a few weeks' time another difficult element was added. Little Aunt Robinson arrived on the scene, full of zeal for seeing the sights, dabbling in politics, and with much the same circle of French and Russian friends as Lady Malmesbury! "I wonder how it will answer!" wrote Lady Frances to her faithful Cozens.

Perhaps if she had seen the pressing invitation sent by Lady Malmesbury to this same Mrs. Robinson, she would not have felt so apprehensive. And as the letter gives a sparkling account of Paris under unique circumstances I will transcribe it.

"It is impossible to conceive anything as amusing or interesting as this place at this moment in every way, but especially the spectacle of the town full of the troops of all nations without any apparent enmity, and everything going on in a common way. The Guards relieving alternately, Austrian, Prussian, Russian and National. . . . You must be satisfied with my *journal*[1] unless you will *come and see me here*. I really think it is as superior to my expectations as it is possible to be. And altogether

[1] Her letters went the round of her family.

Paris would seem as well worth coming to for a person who like you did not care about the society.

"The kindness and attention of all my French friends is really more delightful and flattering than I can express. They are all devoted to me. Olivier de Vérac thinks of nothing but seeing me all the day long, so does Robert Fagel [he was Minister to the King of the Netherlands]. Mme. de Catuelan and all Olivier's family. . . . Bowles is also entirely our cavalier. Michel Woronzow [commanding the Russian army of occupation] breakfasted with me this morning. . . .

"The English swarm here as you may suppose. Lowry and Lord and Lady Grantham live entirely with them. He has a moderate house, dreadfully noisy, as mine is, but if you come, let me know in time, as I mean to change and could get you into the same place I go to and where Harry [Lord Palmerston] will be also, and we might *club* as to horses, etc.

"Lowry has the worst English cook I ever saw. To-day I give Bowles a dinner and we are going to the [Théâtre] Français. Michel [Woronzow] is going to drive us about in his droschki *and real Russian horses*!

"I stick to the foreigners as much as possible and mean to squeeze myself into as many French houses as I can, and see all the lions."

Could a travelled citizen of the world with so keen a taste for events as Mrs. Robinson resist such an invitation, even though she had no escort, almost an essential protection in those days for old or young? But Lady Malmesbury sent a faithful foot-

PARIS AFTER THE RESTORATION

man, Henri, to meet her and her chaise at Calais and she arrived safely on October 28th at Paris, and divided her time between Lady Malmesbury and the Hôtel d'Abrantès.

"Little Aunt Robinson" also kept a diary. She also preserved the invitation cards she received. One supposes she thought it would be pleasant to have mementoes of the many entertainments given by the Allies to each other; of the great ball given by the Duchess of Wellington or those of Lady Castlereagh, or General Barnes, or Lord Hill, or the select parties where Mme. de Duras received a favoured few every evening, her husband, the Duc de Duras, being "*premier gentilhomme de la maison du roi*".

Lady Malmesbury went to the Hôtel de Wagram in the Rue de la Paix with Miss Temple for company, though each took her own way. Lady Malmesbury had many old friends among the foreigners assembled in Paris, but most of all among the French noblesse of the *ancien régime*. She was far more in sympathy with them than with her own countryfolk and usually adopted their point of view. She plunged at once, on her arrival at the Hôtel de Wagram, into the politics of the hour, as her diary shows.

"Madame de la Coste came to me directly, very much dissatisfied with all that is going on, and told me that Talleyrand had wished the King not to return to Paris till everything was properly done, and then to come back without odium, but that '*we all* thought he was not to be trusted, which we are not sure of now'."

Her most intimate friends in Paris were in the family circle and among the relatives of the Marquis and Marquise de Vérac, the latter a daughter of the Comte de Noailles. There she was in the midst of a society which still retained the charm of the *ancien régime* and which was in close contact with the court. There she heard of the royalist hopes for the dismissal of Fouché, and the latest gossip about the royal family, also their fears that Marshal Ney, then awaiting his trial for high treason, might be spared; and she burned with a desire to see the King himself and to give him some good advice. During his days of exile she had been a good friend to him and a frequent correspondent. She had apparently no difficulty in obtaining her wish.

"*Monday, 14th August.*—I had my audience with the King. He received me with the greatest kindness, and we had a great deal of the most interesting conversation. I exhorted him with all my power to be firm and sure. I said, '*Pensez, Sire, à la distance qu'il y a entre le caractère de Bonaparte et l'extrême bonté de votre Majesté. Il faut tenir le juste milieu. Je crains votre bonté, je l'avoue, et si l'on ne punit pas les traîtres, et surtout ce Ney, vous ne serez jamais en sécurité. Au reste, la main de Dieu est visible dans tous les événements passés. L'année dernière, Il a remis cet homme entre les mains de ses ennemis pour qu'on lui fasse justice. On ne l'a pas assez faite. Une seconde fois Il le leur a redonné, et ce sera agir contre les conseils de la prudence que de laisser échapper les coquins qui pourraient ramener les maux passés. J'espère que nous pourrons le tenir en sûreté. Songez à la distance d'entre le caractère de Bonaparte et celui de votre Majesté, et au moins prenez le milieu.*'

PARIS AFTER THE RESTORATION

"He answered very gravely, '*Soyez tranquille, je saurai faire mon devoir. Je serai juste, je vous en donne ma parole d'honneur.*'

"He talked about Bonaparte and said, '*Il est plus sécure à Ste-Hélène qu'à Elbe*'. He then added what Lord Castlereagh had told me, that in case of Bonaparte's death his body was to be brought back to France to convince the French that he was dead. Upon my saying I thought there might have been a better measure still than Ste-Hélène, he said, '*Oui*, St. Pancras Churchyard'.

"He highly praised the Duke of Wellington and I told him that the Duke was even more proud of the good conduct of his troops than of their valour. '*Partout où j'ai passé*' (said he) '*on me criait, "Vivent les bons Anglais!" Et vous sentez bien que je n'ai pas désiré les contredire!*' He embraced me at entering and retiring and nothing could be more friendly and kind. Poor man! He looks careworn in the face and is dragged different ways by Fouché and his partisans and his old natural character and by unwise advisers. . . ."

Fouché, hated by the royalists, was held in absolute abhorrence by Madame d'Angoulême, that tragic victim of fate whose soul was so seared by the execution of her parents and all the horrors of her imprisonment in the Temple that she could not forgive the fickle Parisian crowds who welcomed her so warmly, or receive their plaudits but with ill-concealed tears and shudders. A strong, harsh character, she refused to compromise even at the King's bidding. Lady Malmesbury records an instance of this:

"The King had a scene with Madame la Duchesse d'Angoulême about the signature of Fouché's marriage contract. [He married Mademoiselle de Castellane, an heiress who was very much in love with him.] '*Madame, vous avez réfusé de signer le contrat d'un de mes ministres! Il me semble que si je l'ai signé, le reste de ma famille l'aurait dû faire aussi.*' To which she very properly replied, '*Il est impossible, Sire, que la fille de Louis XVI signe le contrat d'un de ses meurtriers*'."

Paris was at her most brilliant in the summer of 1815. Cloudless skies, masses of flowers everywhere combined to increase the pleasure of the gay cosmopolitan crowds collected there for business or amusement. There were reviews, royal ceremonies, balls, concerts, routs, given by Lady Castlereagh, by the Duke of Wellington, the Duchess of Richmond, Lady Kinnaird and many others. There were delightful expeditions to St. Cloud, Malmaison, Versailles, Meudon and other palaces lately occupied by Napoleon's large family of kings and queens.

But though the surface of things seemed unruffled and the Parisians bore their trials for the most part stoically, there were many hidden causes of anxiety. Not that the French for the most part either regretted Napoleon or ardently desired the return of Louis XVIII, whose ignoble flight to Ghent during the Hundred Days had discredited him in their eyes. But the royalists were dissatisfied, suspicious and jealous. Those who had spent the best years of life in exile and had impoverished themselves in the royal cause now found them-

PARIS AFTER THE RESTORATION

selves in a less good position than others of their class who had compromised and served Napoleon. They were naturally indignant that such men as Talleyrand and Fouché, murderers of Louis XVI, should with the approval of the Allies be placed in power, and the King obliged to rule through them.

Among the royalists the extremists, who called themselves *royalistes purs*, demanded the impossible, that is to say, a return to the state of things existing in pre-revolution times.

Most dangerous were the Jacobins, a survival of the days of the Terror, which was still vividly before men's memories. They constituted an ever-present danger which rumbled beneath the surface like a hidden volcano and was feared by all parties alike.

France, as Guizot says in his memoirs, on the verge of bankruptcy, at the end of her resources in men and money, only desired peace and liberty. In fifteen years Napoleon had made more treaties of peace than any other king, yet never had war broken out so often or peace proved more of a delusion. Peace and liberty appeared with the Restoration. War was neither a necessity nor a passion for the Bourbons.

The Allies entered Paris ostensibly as friends, in reality as conquerors, determined to contract the swollen boundaries of France, to exact a proper indemnity and to demand the restitution of their stolen works of art. English, Russian, Austrian, Prussian and Dutch armies were encamped in and around the capital. Foreign regiments were often to be seen marching through the streets changing to fresh quarters, where they were always unwelcome.

Friction was inevitable, and even the English and Dutch, so popular at first on account of their excellent discipline, became before long a source of irritation to the French; while the Prussians and Austrians, especially the former, earned their undying hatred from their cruelty and from the way they robbed and destroyed, Blücher himself showing the example to his subordinates.

In the meantime the poor King seems to have been popular with nobody. Lady Frances's diary shows this:

"*Tuesday, 15th.*—Went to hear the King's *Messe* on a *jour de fête*. Got there late owing to a mistake in the message, but we were allowed to wait in the passage and we saw the Royal family pass. With the exception of Monsieur,[1] a most wretched, ignoble set! Madame d'Angoulême looked harassed and ill. She set out the same morning for the South, where she and her husband are popular and have a good deal of influence. The King in passing showed himself to the people in the gardens. There were some acclamations, which, however, proceeded more from the women than the men, and gave one but little idea of coming from the heart of a people who have cheered whatever was offered to them for the last twenty-five years! The King's infirmities and heavy make are a constant theme of ridicule, forming as they do a contrast to the fine figure and studied magnificence of Bonaparte. A few days back some wags dressed up a hog with the ribbon and insignia of the St. Esprit, hid the animal amongst them while they drove it forward calling

[1] Later Charles X.

out '*Vive le Roi!*' and then, dispersing, left it in the midst of the street!

"Dined at Lord Stewart's. An immense dinner which ended in a ball, and though handsome in itself, tedious and tiresome from its length. Talleyrand came there for a short time, but I had no opportunity of hearing him converse, which I should have liked. I never saw a worse countenance and it certainly does not belie him."

She was better pleased apparently with Fouché, whom she saw at Lord Castlereagh's ball. She describes him thus:

"A little thin man with an intelligent countenance, married *for love* to a Mademoiselle de Castellane of one of the first families in France. A young and rather pretty woman.

"*Sunday*, 22*nd*.—The Duke of Wellington dined with us—not in very good spirits—it was said there were some *désagréments* going on. He spoke with much openness and simplicity of himself. He said he had last year, while ambassador here, received many notices of intentions to assassinate him. Among the rest a message from Lady Yarmouth, telling him *the Marshals* would take care of him, a protection which he observed he was not very ambitious of securing. He seemed to have no doubt they would have prevented his leaving Paris, and he said it was very lucky he was gone to Vienna.

"*Saturday*, 26*th*.—Lowry's Division reviewed by the Duke, the Emperors of Russia and Austria, and the King of Prussia. The 'dandy' Emperor with much bad taste chose to drill two regiments of his own on the ground just before the two Brigades, so that we had to wait above two hours! The Review, however, went off well and the Duke expressed his admiration."

Lady Frances relates her impressions in a letter to Miss Cozens as follows:

"You may easily conceive that, being here for the express purpose of seeing everything, we lead a most hurried life, and though it is of itself productive of great amusement I own I find it fatiguing and I shall be very glad if we remain on here to retire to my villa at Neuilly.

"I can, however, tell you a little of the life we lead, one which is in every respect so new to me that I have not yet been able to get at all used to it, and continually feel I must awake from it as from a dream! But I should indeed be ungrateful if I did not do justice to Lowry's unceasing kindness and affection, and as I know your anxiety for my happiness, my dearest Co., I know it will give you pleasure to hear this.

"Though we have lost no time in seeing the sights, we have yet made but little progress when the whole is considered. The more I see of the ornamental parts of the town, the more beautiful I think it. Nothing can surpass the *coup d'œil* of the Louvre, the Tuileries, the Place Louis XV and the Champs-Élysées, all lying together and ended on one side by very handsome houses and on the other side by the river, which is lined with fine quays ornamented by handsome bridges. The centre of the Tuileries and of the Champs Élysées filled with good trees.

PARIS AFTER THE RESTORATION

"To English eyes not the least gratifying part of the sight is to see our troops encamped there, occupying it with all the moderation and discipline that they have shown throughout the whole campaign. Doing no mischief but what the presence of lines and tents must occasion. Never getting into any quarrel with the inhabitants. The same thing is repeated at Neuilly, where Lowry has got for his billet the Palace of the Princess Borghese[1] and where we intend to retire after the Granthams leave us if the army is not moved, which is not improbable. The house is a very large one and the place now filled by a camp must have been pretty. The house was unfurnished last year and has but a scanty supply now, but it must have had all the *luxe* of a magnificent and profligate woman, for a few paces from the house was a pavilion hid from every other part, magnificently furnished, which was the retreat of the lady when she chose to be in private.

"But of all the luxury and magnificence I ever saw, that which we went to yesterday surpasses everything—St. Cloud and Versailles! The former was Bonaparte's constant residence and is in itself a very pretty place in the old French style of alleys and fountains, but it stands in an uneven and pretty country on the banks of the Seine, which gives it a natural beauty in spite of the distortions of art. The house is as magnificent as gilding, pictures and statues can make it. The private apartments, particularly Bonaparte's, have an appearance of comfort. It is, however, surpassed a

[1] Napoleon's sister, Pauline, whose house in Paris has for long been the British Embassy.

hundredfold by Versailles, which bears the impress of Louis XIV's magnificence, as do the gardens with their marble reservoirs for the waterworks, the number of marble and bronze statues and above all the superb orangerie. The Trianons are *à l'anglaise* and a very pretty imitation of our villas. . . .

"You can easily suppose how all these places brought back to one's mind the history of the unfortunate Marie-Antoinette and all the horrors of the revolution! They seemed quite present when one of the Swiss Guard who had been there at the time shewed us the private door through which she escaped to the King's apartments on the night when the populace broke into the Palace of Versailles, the balcony on which she showed herself with the Dauphin in her arms, and the staircase upon which two of the Garde du Corps were killed in endeavouring to defend her.

"Everything indeed in this town has been marked by such extraordinary events that I cannot shake off the impression. The Champs de Mars, the Place du Carrousel, the Place Louis XV, where the King was beheaded, the windows of the Tuileries where he was continually, and even the very lanterns hanging about, recall the horrors of those times and in spite of all its beauty give one a sort of antipathy to the place and people.

"Paris is at this moment perfectly quiet, but very ill-disposed, I believe, towards the King, whom they laugh at and despise. The presence of the foreign armies is dreadfully galling to them and the general appearance of the bettermost class of men whom you see walking about is gloomy and *soucieux*. As to what political arrangements are

PARIS AFTER THE RESTORATION

going on, we know much less than you in England. The Ancien Régime abuse the government as I hear from my mother, who sees a good deal of the Véracs, but on the other hand the King's situation is allowed to be a difficult one. Fouché is still the principal person. Marshal Ney is taken, but what will be done with him is not known. La Bédoyère, who was the first Colonel to take his regiment over to Bonaparte, is on trial, but that is kept secret and it is only conjectured that he is to be shot. . . .

"*August 21st,* 1815.—For the last two days I have been at the Louvre, fearing that the pictures might be gone before I could see them. For the Bavarians, Prussians and Spaniards are taking away what was stolen from them and have already got about a hundred. I think this mortification of their vanity chafes the French more than anything, particularly when inflicted by the Germans whom they detest. . . . The discipline of our army has secured to us much more good-will and we have the additional advantage of not having a legal claim upon any of the ornaments of their capital and I fear the Duke will be too moderate to take any trophy of his glory.

"The spoliation, or rather the restitution, of stolen goods is going on in this capital and excites prodigious indignation among the French, whose vanity is wounded in the most susceptible spot. The Duke's wonted popularity is quite at an end and they abuse him as much as they worshipped him before. And all this because as C.-in-C. of the Belgian army he sent some English soldiers to protect the workmen in the Louvre.

"Yesterday the Austrians took the Venetian horses and to-day they say they are to take the pillar which is made of Austrian cannon. The whole of course produces the greatest sensation. But never was anything to equal my mother's violence on this subject. She almost goes beyond the French themselves, as I *hear*, for, partly thanks to Fanny Temple, who gave her a hint, and partly from knowing that Lowry would take up the cudgels pretty warmly in defence of the Duke, she has had self-command enough not to enter on the discussion in this house...."

Lady Malmesbury was nothing if not a partisan, and besides this, for some reason I have not been able to discover, disliked the Duke. She never lost a chance of saying something spiteful about him.

On the subject of the restitution of the works of art, she took the side of her French friends and was told all the details which seemed intended to offend and humiliate Louis XVIII. She did not realise that the King was obliged to take the line he did in apparently yielding to force for fear of incurring unpopularity with his subjects. Talleyrand engineered the affair most skilfully so that the odium fell on the Duke.

Lady Malmesbury's diary gives an account of it:

"Apsley [Lord Bathurst's son], whom I met dining at Fanny's [Lady F. Cole], said we had signed a Convention by which we were to take all the pictures and statues and restore them to their original owners, *including the Pope*, to whom we were also to give £6,000 to cover the expense of carriage! The superlative absurdity of all this equals that of the rest of the proceeding. Champcenetz (Governor of the Tuileries) came to me and said that on the preceding day the National Guard on duty at the Galeries du Louvre came to take his orders, saying that a number of men had come and had demanded a considerable number of pictures, which they, according to their duty, had refused to give up without a royal order. Champcenetz immediately went to the King. He, with his usual mildness, said that, though he could not consent to the measure, there was no resisting force, for the men had said their orders were to beat down the doors and take the pictures by force. And the King told Champcenetz to give the order for removal. No comment is necessary as to the indecency of this proceeding...

"It was a pity that the claimants were not satisfied with their own property. The Dutch seem to have been far from modest in their views and the Prussians were positively dishonest! Champcenetz said to Miss Temple [Lord Palmerston's sister] later, that, after what had happened, he conceived that the most decent mode of proceeding was to shut up the gallery while the thing was doing, that he had accordingly put up a placard to that effect. Very soon, however, he received a message from the Prussian governor of the town, to say that the galleries must be thrown open to the public, that they might see it was done by force, and a guard of English soldiers there for the purpose (sent there by the Duke's orders). There never was such an outrage to a Sovereign in his own Palace.... It has tarnished Lord Wellington's laurels and the glory of the battle of Waterloo is effaced by the storming of the Louvre....

"The Gallery is in such a state of plunder that

Monsieur de la Bourdonnaye saw a Prussian officer walking with two women who were admiring two little pictures. '*Voulez-vous les avoir?*' he said, and forthwith unhooked them. Each woman put one in her shawl and walked off!

"I find the Prussians have so completely cleared the Musée d'Artillerie that they have taken even the armour of Bayard and Francis I, etc., to which even the English cannot pretend they have any right!"

The Hôtel d'Abrantès was particularly gay just at that time, for Lady Georgina Bathurst, a special young friend of Lady Frances, was paying her a visit, and to amuse her the Coles kept open house to the many young people, mostly men, whose duty, no less than pleasure, kept them in Paris.

One day, November 7th, Mrs. Robinson, who had an instinct for recording events picturesquely, tells how she and a gay party consisting of the Coles, Lady Georgina, Major Bowles and Captain Hutchinson made an expedition to Fontainebleau, spending a night there at the Hôtel de la Galerie, where their party was increased by the Duke of Richmond and his daughter with Lord Apsley and Seymour Bathurst.

The Palace was thoroughly visited and they made long drives through the forest, which was much admired, though the woods were considered inferior either to the New Forest or Park Place, Lord Malmesbury's small country house near Henley. But it was a delightful expedition and Aunt Robinson "celebrated" it. In the midst of a solemn circle —shall we call it the Hôtel d'Abrantès circle?—

PARIS AFTER THE RESTORATION

formed round the Roche de St. Germain in the forest, a seedling birch-tree was carefully uprooted and carried away to be in due time put into the earth at Durnford, her country home in Wiltshire. Finally it was planted in a conspicuous position "on the left side of the lawn from the bow window and near the gravel walk by the river" on the great occasion, October 15th, 1818, when the Allies met in Congress at Aix-la-Chapelle to finish their work in France by deciding to remove the remains of the armies of occupation by November 30th, 1818.

CHAPTER XII

WITH THE ARMY OF OCCUPATION IN FRANCE

THE question that agitated Sir Lowry's mind was that of his immediate prospects. The more remote future also claimed thought. He was far from rich and the duties of his present position were costly. It was probable that the armies would soon be moved from Paris. The Duke had done his best for him by giving him the command of the army of occupation to be quartered on the northern frontier of France. A general peace was hoped for and seemed probable, and that being so, what would be the fate of the many brilliant soldiers with nothing to do and all hoping for employment?

Lord Malmesbury discusses the matter in his letters to his daughter and is ready to use his very considerable influence with the Duke of York and also with the Regent himself to obtain the promise of a "government", not as a simple favour but as an acknowledgment of Sir Lowry's brilliant services. But that lay in the future. For the moment the interest was centred on whether the next few months would take him and Lady Frances to Cambrai or Valenciennes.

Lord Malmesbury writes on December 28th, 1815:

"If you and Lowry are not sent home, I scarce know what to wish about your future residence.

CATHERINE GERTRUDE HARRIS
Married, 1785, Honble. Frederick Robinson

HARRIET
daughter of Sir George Amyand, Bart.
Married, 1771, James, first Earl of Malmesbury

[*From the picture by Romney*]

ARMY OF OCCUPATION IN FRANCE

Georgy [Lady G. Bathurst], who called here yesterday, gives such a pleasant and comfortable description of your house and society at Paris that perhaps the best would be your remaining on in the Hôtel d'Abrantès till April, and then to be ordered home. Georgy is delightful about her travels and speaks in the most feeling manner of the reception you gave her and so do both Lord and Lady Bathurst. You have a very comfortable *chez-nous* and the enjoyment of a party *en famille*; for when at Cambrai —if you go there—you will seldom have this satisfaction."

He wrote on December 15th, 1815:

"I do not know whether to be glad or sorry that you are likely to inhabit Cambrai. There is much to be said in both ways. Cambrai is much more in the country and I believe cheaper than Paris. It is also 60 or 70 miles nearer Calais. The environs are pleasant and the town itself very good, larger, I should think, than Winchester and much pleasanter."

Early in 1816 Sir Lowry took up his command at Cambrai. Of the British army of occupation 27,000 quitted France; 30,000 remained under his command. The Duke's headquarters were transferred to Cambrai. I feel sure that my grandmother preferred her home at Cambrai, where she had a good house and a garden, to any of the gaieties of Paris. Gardening was a favourite occupation in her family. Her father alludes to this. In March 1816 he writes:

"Catherine [her sister] seems much pleased with Cambrai and gives me a most comfortable account of you and Lowry. I daresay the garden you are laying out will live on long in the annals of Cambrai as the one I made at Berlin did in the annals of that capital."

Lady Frances was an accomplished draughtswoman. There is a scrapbook with landscapes of her travels painted by her with a few by other people. The first in the book is a delicate sepia wash of the house at Cambrai in 1818—a typical French house with a high-pitched roof and mansards, only two floors. In the same book there is a plan of Cambrai published locally, showing the *enceinte* of the walls and the citadel, for Cambrai was an important fortress in those days. There was a cathedral and several religious houses and some factories for the manufacture of the "cambric" so popular in England. Now, so far as I can make out from the plan in the Guide Bleu, the citadel is used as a barracks and the walls have become public walks and gardens. On the map of 1816 the quarters of all the Staff are marked: Sir Lowry's was No. 1 in the Rue de Poissonier near the Cathedral and close to the Duke's house, which must have been convenient as he was very good-natured about lending it to Lady Frances when her own was too full. I quote his letter:

"My dear Lady Frances, *March 25th, 1817*
I received your letter yesterday evening, and I beg you to make what use you please of my quarters at Cambray whenever it can be con-

venient to you. Even if I return to that country in a short time, which is not probable, I should go to Mont St. Martin, and the house at Cambray would be at your service. I am glad to hear Miss Cole is so well and I hope you are so likewise. I don't like that disposition for flirting!
    Believe me
           Ever yours most sincerely,
                  WELLINGTON"

"Miss Cole", my grandparents' first child, had been born in June 1816, but not at Cambrai. Lady Frances went to London for her confinement to her father's house in Hill Street at his wish, and no doubt it was greatly to his happiness having his Fan-Fan with him. He took a special interest in this baby, as did also Lady Malmesbury. She was their first granddaughter, Lord Fitz-Harris' children being boys.

This is a letter from Sir George Murray, A.A.G., to Lady Frances Cole, written from Paris, where he was apparently on duty with his Corps Commander:

"DEAR LADY FRANCES,   6*th April*, 1816
    How great an advantage a Lady's correspondence has over a gentleman's! Sir Lowry bores one about the moving of a regiment and about a Barracks Regulation, subjects to which he may be dull enough to attach some importance at Cambray. But in Paris a letter about a Cap to be bought in the Passage de l'Aisne is far more interesting and more certain of being attended to!

I shall go about your commission this morning and shall do my best to equal Sir Lowry in taste.

As to *price*, however, you must expect to pay at least double, for I have no chance single-handed against a Marchande de Modes! Indeed, I think Sir Lowry owed half his success to my modesty, for I was so much ashamed of his bargaining that I was forced to go out of the shop, from which the woman supposed we were going off altogether and instantly came down in her demands! My manœuvre will turn probably to my own confusion, however, when I am without a well-practised second capable of turning it to account.

You were extremely welcome to make the use you did of my house for your aunt and cousins. As there seems such a want of other accommodation, I shall offer the same use of it to the Erskines, who talk of setting out for Brussels on Monday. Although, indeed, if we make a general move about that time I shall be at a loss how to give up my house, but as I propose dining with an Irish friend I may possibly find a night's lodging under the table!

Believe me very sincerely yours,

G. Murray"

Cambrai became very gay under the auspices of the British soldier, who insists always on having his favourite amusement, sport, to lighten the monotony of military life. Captain George Bowles, who had survived Waterloo, and was now encamped with his regiment of Guards at Cambrai, writes to Mrs. Robinson to tell her all about it:

"I ought long before this to have written to you, not only to inform you of my safe arrival in this happy town but to have thanked you for all your kindness to me when on your side of the water. I have now another inducement, having to wish you joy of the safe arrival of a *niece*, and pray let me make you the vehicle of my congratulations to Sir Lowry and Lady Frances. *He* would, I suppose, have rather been introduced to a future G.C.B., but that may happen yet in due time. . . .

"This place has been, till the day before yesterday, as gay as possible. We have had one incessant round of parties by day and night. The departure of headquarters to Paris and that of the Richmonds [the Duke of R. and his family] for Brussels has reduced us to a state of comparative torpor.

"It is quite impossible to imagine any schoolboy in higher spirits or up to any sort of fun than the Duke of Wellington. He has just taken a large chateau about twelve miles from hence, which he means to make his headquarters on his return from Paris, where he talks of passing the whole of this month. His plans on the subject of the said chateau are quite '*en prince*'. He has sent for a pack of hounds and as we are to be encamped as soon as the harvest is over in that neighbourhood he will have reviews and '*chasses*' alternately. Everything is perfectly tranquil in this country. . . ."

The same to the same.

CAMBRAI
August 12th, 1816

"My frisk to Bruxelles and to Waterloo was a very interesting one. Very few indications now remain there of the 18th June, 1815: excepting at Hougoumont and La Haye Sainte, you would not guess you were on a field of battle. The crops are, as may be supposed, particularly luxuriant. Bruxelles is flourishing with the money that ought to be expended in England. It is quite lamentable to see the numbers of our countrymen and women who are living there and the quantities of lace, etc., etc., which is smuggled by their means is hardly to be believed. And all this at a time when our own manufacturers are literally starving! . . .

The 'Monsieurs' have behaved very well of late and are much improved in their manners since we took the liberty of disarming the National Guard of this town, and I have no doubt we shall now remain quite as good friends as is agreeable during the rest of our stay here. . . ."

On August 24th, 1817, a son—Arthur Lowry Cole—was born. The event took place in London. There is nothing much otherwise to chronicle this year; visitors came and went, Lady Malmesbury paid a visit, and Lady Frances gave balls and parties. Sir Lowry had some greyhounds sent out and the Duke's was not the only pack.

Mr. Creevey also paid a flying visit to Cambrai in 1817–18 and dined with the G.O.C. He says he liked Lady Frances very much, that she was very good-looking, had an excellent manner and was agreeable. He also in another place in his journal pays a tribute to Sir Lowry's independence of character on the occasion of a bill being brought up to the House of Commons to take the Queen's name out of the State prayers:

"It has given me great pleasure to see Sir Lowry's

name stand next to mine in the list of the division. To someone who talked to him while we were dividing he said, he had never had but one opinion as to the impropriety of striking the Queen's name out of the Liturgy, and he was glad he could express his opinion by his vote. Upon my word the gentlemanly conduct of these soldiers, Lord Howard and Sir Lowry Cole, both dependent in a great degree on the Crown, is quite touching! They leave your independent squires a hundred miles behind them."

From Lady Frances to Miss Cozens.

Mont St. Martin
January 16th, 1818

"We came here on Wednesday and in the evening Arthur became a compleat Christian. The frock and cap were both made to fit him very well. Being of a more respectable age, and I must be fain to own a prettier child than Florence ever was, he became them both very much and looked very nice. The Duke of course stood in person. The Duchess of Richmond represented Lady Grantham and Mr. Craddock Enniskillen. As Arthur had been baptised, and there was no water in question, he did not think it necessary to cry, but amused himself with laughing at the candles all the time. Thus the great ceremony is over and I am glad of it."

Though the "Monsieurs", as Captain Bowles ungrammatically called the French, were on the whole, if not friendly to the English soldiers, inoffensive, this was not always the case. Lady

Malmesbury on one occasion heard the Duke give an account of how he had been insulted the day before. A man came up to him as if to prevent him from passing. He was arrested and sent to the Guardhouse. The Duke went out boar-hunting and on his return a man came quite close alongside and *grunted*, which is the French mode of insulting an officer, meaning to express "*Cochon*". The Duke next morning had an interview with the Procureur du Roi and explained to him that hitherto he had forbidden his officers who wore their sidearms to avenge insults, and that it would be very unpleasant at this period of affairs to be obliged to *order them to use them*!—This man told him that a Vendéen regiment had had to be removed from Lille on account of the eternal quarrels between them and the townspeople.

One of the difficult incidents which concerned a regiment of the Guards forming part of the British garrison arose out of the attempt on the Duke's life made by a French ex-sergeant of Dragoons, by name Cantillon, in Paris on February 10th, 1818. The Duke was returning from a dinner-party towards midnight in his coach. As he drove into the courtyard of his house in the Rue des Champs-Élysées, this man fired at him and fortunately missed him. He got away under cover of the darkness, but enquiries and a trial established his identity and revealed a widespread plot against the Duke's life, which had originated among the French refugees in Brussels, many of them ex-soldiers of Napoleon's army. But, though enquiries and trials took place, no one was punished. The mysterious part of the affair was that for days or even weeks before Cantillon fired his shot at the Duke, a rumour spread over Valenciennes, Cambrai and other places occupied by the British that he had been already assassinated. But this report had not obviously reached Sir Lowry's ears or those of his Staff. After the attempted murder the French police were very zealous in their investigations and made these the excuse for creating unpleasantness with the officers of the Guards, who had their club in the house of a Mr. Wright. They were much surprised and angered when the French police forced their way into the club and made, as the members considered, insulting enquiries; so much so that they refused to allow them to continue. Monsieur de la Tour (Prefect) and the police carried the matter to the Duke, obviously making very unpleasant insinuations against the regiment.

The Duke to Sir Lowry Cole.

PARIS
February 26th, 1818

"MY DEAR COLE,

Sir George Murray communicated to me your letter of the 20th and I had a conversation with Monsieur de Caze [1] upon the subject. He has heard from Monsieur de la Tour. His report does not differ materially from yours. It appears that he understood that Mr. Wright was a sort of Restaurateur and therefore liable to the jurisdiction of the police in the ordinary way without going through the forms which are necessary when a person belonging to the army of occupation is to appear before a French authority. I explained Mr.

[1] Prime Minister to Louis XVIII.

Wright's situation to Monsieur de Caze and the circumstances complained of will not occur again.

There had been reports at Cambray and Valenciennes and all over the Departments of the North that I was assassinated some days before the attempt was made or could be known in these places—that is, from the 8th to the 13th—and the Government have been anxious to trace these reports to their source as one mode of discovering who made the attempt and who were his accomplices. It appears that Capel the tailor says that he heard the report in the club of the Guards. This is impossible, as I believe no tailor frequents the club. However, it is only desirable that that matter should be ascertained and that Capel should be made to say from whom he heard it. I am sure the officers of the Guards will not refuse permission to the continuation of these enquiries to trace the report to its source. Indeed, they cannot refuse it, as it is obvious that such conduct would be to oppose themselves to the course taken by the justice of the country to discover a criminal, and the consequence would be that in any similar case in the future the conspirators possibly would only have to say, 'I had it from a British officer of the Guards' to put an end to proceedings.

I beg you to explain this to the Commanding Officer of the Guards and to settle between him and Monsieur de la Tour in what manner the enquiry shall continue. The most probable thing is that Capel did not hear the report from the club and that no officer of the Guards ever heard it or mentioned it. But it is desirable that this should be ascertained and that Capel the tailor should be

dealt with by the police, as they may think proper, till he states where he did really hear a report which, it appears, has been traced to him.
Ever yours most sincerely,
WELLINGTON"

Sir Lowry answered:

CAMBRAY
1st March, 1818
"MY DEAR LORD,
I have received your letter of the 26th inst., and I trust Your Grace did not for a moment imagine that there could be any objection or wish on the part of the officers of the Guards to prevent or throw any impediment to the tracing of the original report of an attempt against your life, and I do hope you could still less suppose that I could countenance such a proceeding!

What the officers of the Guards objected to was the manner of proceeding on the part of the police and the questions put by them to Mr. Wright—which they at present deny—as it appeared to insinuate that the report originated with them, which I have no hesitation in saying was the wish and object of Monsieur de la Tour and the police of this place should be believed!

On receiving Your Grace's letter, I communicated the contents to Colonel Woodford of the Guards, who at my desire waited on Monsieur Latour and told him the officers of the club were willing and had been so to give him all the assistance he could desire in tracing the report.

It was, I understand, talked of at the club, as everything will be, and has been traced to a tailor man of the name of Capel, who keeps the public-house near your house. He says that the report was mentioned in his house on the 5th or 6th, he cannot say by whom.

Lt. Campbell, who was A.D.C. to Sir A. Adair when with the army, and who is now in Paris, heard it at the Post House here on the 5th, but from whom I do not know or whether from an English or Frenchman. Lt. Campbell is at present in Paris, but where I do not know.

I have only to add that Monsieur Latour shall get every information we can supply on the subject.

And with the sincerest wishes for your safety,
Believe me, my dear Lord,
Yours, etc.
G. LOWRY COLE"

From the Duke to Sir Lowry.

PARIS
"MY DEAR COLE, March 5th, 1818
I have received your letter of the 1st and you may depend on it I had no meaning in the letter which I wrote you on the 16th, which was not clearly expressed. I stated my opinion that Monsieur de la Tour was wrong in the mode in which he endeavoured to trace a report in the club of the Guards, but that the officers of the Guards could not object to his tracing a report through the club without stopping the course of justice. This I could not suppose they had any intention of doing, much less that you encouraged them in doing so.
Ever yours,
WELLINGTON"

Lady Malmesbury describes her visit to Cambrai in 1818:

ARMY OF OCCUPATION IN FRANCE

"*Saturday, May 23rd.*—Left Paris at half-past eight. Slept at Roye—eleven and a quarter hours. Bad inn—very noisy.

"*Sunday, May 24th.*—Left Roye at eight and was stopped at the gates of Peronne one hour for the procession of the Holy Sacrament. Hot and windy. Arrived at Cambrai at a quarter past four."

And there she stayed for six weeks or so. She must have thoroughly enjoyed herself, for there were dinner-parties every night, either at home or at one of the families quartered at Cambrai, a great deal of informal society and incessant callers, so even her thirst for society must have been quenched. There were visits to Lord Hill's country place just outside the town and frequent intercourse with the Duke, whom she evidently liked much better now that he had more time to make himself agreeable to her. She describes a review of the Russian troops at Maubeuge:

"Left Cambrai at half-past ten o'clock. Were detained for hours at Bavet and did not get to Maubeuge till half-past one or nearly two. Country ugly. Fine crops of wheat, barley forward, rye nearly ripe. Quantities of Colza and poppies for oil.

"*June 1st.*—Fine day. Fanny and Anne to the review. I was unwell and did not go. Dined at Michel Worontzoff's and sat next the Grand Duke. He is not good-looking, but is civil with a coarse, rough manner. We dined in a large temporary room with all the Staff officers of both armies here. Beautiful bands playing. During the evening dancing and Russian national music. The band playing and singing at once, and especially a particular dance composed for a fête given by Potemkin to the Empress Catherine at the Taurida palace. A mazurka was danced remarkably well by Narischkin, a Monsieur de Polignac in the Russian service, a Cathcart and another Russian.

"*June 2nd.*—Very fine and very hot. Went to the review of cavalry. Very fine troops, the horses excellent, and the whole surprising to me who had seen it in so different a state thirty-five years ago [when she was in Russia]. First they all marched and trotted past, then the flying artillery manœuvred, and then there was a charge of Cossacks—very wild and pretty. The ground was a pretty spot with a little prospect from it. Indeed, the country about Maubeuge is very tolerable, undulating with occasional clumps of wood. We went in a *calèche* of Worontzoff's drawn by Russian horses, which went through what one would call an impassable road for a carriage!

"We dined again at Worontzoff's [he commanded the Russian army] and, being the highest in rank, I again sat next the Grand Duke. Nothing could exceed the whole of their attentions to us. We had three A.D.C.'s to attend us, Captain Battie at all parts of the day, Yemouleff and Ravefsky and occasionally Prince Galitzin. All gentlemanlike men and of a better tone than the Russians in general of this time.

"*Wednesday, June 3rd.*—Returned to Cambrai extremely hot and dirty. Driven to Valenciennes by Russian horses—three relays.

"Dined at the Duke of Wellington's. His Staff,

Pozzo di Borgo[1], Mrs. Henry, the Misses Cator and Alava[2]. The Duke told us several anecdotes about Fouché. That at the last conference before Paris in 1815, which lasted till five in the morning, the dispute had been about the King assuming the national colours and the amnesty. To their surprise the next morning Fouché's proclamation was issued, declaring that the Allies would hear of no terms but placing the Bourbons on the throne, of which not a single word had been said. When, after the King's entrance into Paris, Fouché was asked to explain his conduct, he said: '*Vous vouliez le Roi sur le trône. Je l'y ai mis. Qu'est-ce que cela vous fait la manière dont je m'y suis pris?*' Pozzo said it was '*À tout*' [trumps].

"A great dinner to the Waterloo people at the Citadel. In bad taste to have one where so many officers and soldiers in the same garrison had not been there. These officers were of course hurt at it, and it is said the soldiers still more so. The thing which did most harm was the Waterloo medal given to the rank and file, as this seemed to throw all the Peninsula actions so completely in the background, which individually and collectively were in fact far more arduous, and without which Waterloo could never have been fought at all."

Sir Lowry and Lady Frances's house at Cambrai was situated quite near the Cathedral, and evidently

---

[1] This extraordinary adventurer, Corsican and furiously anti-Bonapartist, had after a varied career in secret service and diplomacy become Russian Ambassador at Paris.

[2] Alava, a Spanish general, had served under Wellington in Spain and acquired his friendship. He was at this time Spanish Ambassador to Holland.

there was a pleasant neighbourliness between them and the Bishop, as this charming little letter shows.

From the Archbishop of Cambrai to Lady Frances Cole.

CAMBRAI
26th September, 1818

"M. l'Évêque de Cambrai prie Miladi Frances Cole de lui faire l'honneur d'accepter une boîte d'oignons de tulipes. Tous ne donneront pas fleurs à la prochaine fleuraison. Parmi ceux qui porteront, il y en aura même plusieurs qui ne s'élèveront jusqu'à la hauteur qui leur est propre, qu'après deux ou trois ans. Mais on peut dire d'eux ce que le bon Lafontaine disait de carpillon, 'Petit oignon deviendra grand, pourvu que Dieu lui prête vie'".

Knowing that his command of the British troops in France was to come to an end in 1818, Sir Lowry was very anxious to have a home appointment. He had been on active service for more than twenty years, except for short intervals. Now he was married and had an increasing family, he wished to settle down. No doubt, had his means allowed, he would have left the army and retired to Ireland to the small property left him by his father, where he would have built a house and brought up his children in those country pursuits and business, sport, contested elections and suchlike in which he and his family had always felt such a keen interest.

It was not that his services had not been acknowledged. Three times he had received the thanks of the Government in the House of Commons. After the Battle of Salamanca the K.C.B. was awarded him. But it was the custom to reward officers of distinction in a more practical way. Lord Malmesbury, though not holding office, was much consulted by some of the Tory Ministers and undertook to put forward his claims.

In 1815 Lord Bathurst offered him the governorship of Corfu—rather apologetically; it was obviously not an adequate position for a man of his military rank. It drew from him the following statement of his views:

PARIS
14*th December*, 1815

"MY LORD,

I have had the honour to receive your Lordship's letter of the 7th December, for which I beg to return my most sincere thanks.

Altho' from the tenor of it it is evident that you do not expect me to accept the offer you have been kind enough to make me of the Lt. Governt. of Corfu, it is proof at last that my past services are admitted tho' hitherto unnoticed by H.M.'s Ministers; being the only officer of rank (I believe) who has served with distinction, certainly the only one of my own rank (except the late Sir Thomas Picton) who since my return from the Peninsula has not received some mark of His Royal Highness's approbation. For, however honourable the Bath may be at present, it cannot be denied that it has considerably fallen in value to those who possessed it previous to its new formation.[1]

Hitherto, my Lord, income has not been an object to me, but I confess it to be so at present, having another's comfort and happiness to consider. And as the offer you have been kind enough

[1] Large additions had been made to the number of members.

to make me does not appear desirable in that or any other respect as it stands at present, I beg leave to decline it. Having spent the greatest part of my military life in foreign service, I do not wish to accept any distant situation which does not hold out pecuniary advantages. Besides which, distance may weaken the claims I feel I have on His Majesty's government.

In thus candidly stating my feelings, I beg to assure your Lordship that I am fully sensible of the personal civility I have at all times experienced from you and I should feel great regret if you should feel any part of this personal to yourself.

I have the honour to be, etc., etc.,
G. Lowry Cole"

In September 1816 the governorship of Ceylon, with a salary of £10,000 a year, fell vacant and was offered to Sir Lowry. He hesitated to refuse so good an offer. At the same time he had a rooted objection, as he told Lord Bathurst, to going to India, a prejudice which remained with him all his life. Many years later he prevented his son—also a soldier—from going to India. Acting on Lord Malmesbury's advice, he refused this on the score of his health, which had suffered somewhat from his sojourn in warm climates.

Lord Malmesbury to Sir Lowry Cole.

Hill Street
January 3rd, 1817
"My dear Lowry,

I am entitled to no thanks for my endeavours to promote your interests. You are not only Fanny's husband, but the best of husbands. And knowing you as I do now, had not this tie existed, from personal esteem and affection I should have been most sincerely and truly anxious to see you rewarded in proportion to your repeated and acknowledged services. Your feelings on this point are such as become a high and right-minded man. I understand and admire them perfectly."

The same to the same.

HILL STREET
January 10*th*, 1817

"I saw the Duke of York this morning and stated to him, in a way I am sure you would not disapprove of, your just claims and my natural wishes. Your claims certainly entitled you to one of the best governments, but without waiving that point, I stated you would be ready to accept in the meantime a minor one. The Duke admitted in the handsomest way all I said, spoke of your merits as a soldier in the highest terms of praise, and added that you joined to this the best and rightest heart possible. That he, not only so far as depended on himself, would support but would strongly recommend you. And that he was happy to shew you any proof of esteem and good-will."

CHAPTER XIII

MAURITIUS

IT was no doubt a great disappointment to Sir Lowry that none of the Home Governorships such as Portsmouth or Jersey was offered to him when his command in France came to an end.

Soon after he left Cambrai and brought his family to England, Lord Malmesbury died, thus removing a powerful influence with the government. A peerage was offered, but he considered himself too poor a man to accept an empty honour. His most earnest wish and intention was to provide adequately for his wife and family. Therefore, when in 1823 the governorship of a colony lately brought under British rule was suggested, he felt bound to accept, and he and his whole family embarked in the *Charles Grant* merchantman, bound for the Island of Mauritius, in April 1823.

The islands of Mauritius and Bourbon lay in the trade route to India and the Far East and became therefore of great importance. Early in the eighteenth century the French, requiring a station, not in the Indies but on the route thither, tried Madagascar, but gave it up on account of the unhealthiness of the climate and the hostility of the natives. Finally they transferred their station to the neighbouring islands of Mauritius and Bourbon, whence La Bourdonnais in 1742 and Admiral Suffren in 1782 conducted operations which threatened to

MAURITIUS

win for the French the superiority over the English in the East. The islands became a plotting-ground for the enemies of England, such as discontented Indian potentates, and their creeks and harbours refuges for privateers waiting to attack the East India Fleet.

If Wellesley, Governor-General from 1803 till 1807, could have got his way, these islands, and Ceylon as well, would have been brought under the rule of the East India Company; but his plans were frustrated and it remained to Lord Minto to put an end to these raids by wresting the islands from the French in 1810. In 1815, at the general peace, Bourbon was restored to France, Mauritius with Rodriguez and certain minor dependencies being retained as a Crown Colony.

The Coles brought a retinue of English servants with them—four or five English maids, an Irish gardener from Florence Court who lived with them all his life, a couple of grooms and the usual complement of A.D.C.'s; not to mention their five children.

Sir Lowry Cole writes to Lord Enniskillen telling of their arrival:

PORT LOUIS
"MY DEAREST E., *28th June*, 1823

You will be glad to hear of our safe arrival here after a passage of 77 days or 11 weeks—all well in health. Nothing could be more fortunate than we were in our Captain, who was as accommodating as possible.

I have had so much occupation and have been so little accustomed to business of this nature that I am naturally harassed a good deal, but I have been led to suppose that I have got through the essential part of it with great *éclat*. Fanny writes to Net and has desired her to forward her letter to you. . . .

Letters have been received from India to say that Arthur had applied for leave of absence in order to meet me here. I have not as yet had any letters from him, but I am anxiously looking out for them. I have brought out two horses with me, which promise at present to be very useful. Those to be had in the island are very dear and very indifferent.

Your affec^{ate} Brother,
G. L. Cole"

From Lady F. Cole to Lady Florence Balfour.

1st letter from Mauritius
Port Louis
June 28th, 1823.

"I know it will be with real pleasure, my dearest, that you will hear we are safely arrived at our destination. We reached this port on the 12th of this month, having been exactly eleven weeks at sea. This is reckoned a very good passage and certainly was a much quicker one than I anticipated. We were fortunate in not being becalmed more than a few days under the Line and from thence till we had doubled the Cape we went on most prosperously and without going a mile out of our course, but of course this rapid progress was at the expense of a good deal of rough weather and therefore appeared tedious and tiresome. Off Madagascar we fell in with contrary winds, which buffeted us about nearly in the same spot for twelve or fourteen days. At the end of that time we were overtaken by a most severe thunderstorm, which struck our mainmast, killed an unfortunate sailor and severely hurt the chief mate and another officer, and caused us the only alarm we experienced during the whole voyage. Providentially the ship was not damaged in any way and a few days after we reached this port. . . .

We fortunately made this island early in the morning, so that as we came round it we had an excellent view of it. Its mountains are by no means so bold as those of Madeira, but they are of infinitely more varied and fantastic shapes and, being divided by rich plains, gain height by showing their bases. The whole island is covered with evergreens, woods and almost generally fine verdure . . . which, added to the picturesque outline of the high lands, makes it really beautiful.

This town is situated in an amphitheatre formed by the mountains behind and, being all built of white stone (or wood painted white), with flat roofs and terraces and interspersed with gardens and trees, and the harbour facing it and lined with good quays, has altogether a very fine and very pretty effect.

We anchored in the road at five o'clock in the afternoon, and very soon after Colonel Dumaresq and some other officers came on board. We had arrived sooner than was expected and caused some agitation by our sudden appearance. However, everything was ready for Lowry's reception in form the next day. I preferred following a few hours later when the bustle was a little over, but I understand he was well received and that his *air noble* produced a good effect.

I should find it difficult to describe my own feelings when I first set my foot on shore. They were pleasing and painful, full of regrets yet not without hopes—in short, full of agitation from within and of astonishment from without. The complete novelty of the scene could not but strike anyone. To find oneself surrounded by black and copper-coloured beings, some dressed in the neatness and *recherche* of the Indians, and by far the greater number not dressed at all. To be immediately placed in a palanquin and carried off to the wild cries of the unfortunate slaves, and then to be greeted by the repeated salaams of an old Indian gardener with a long white beard who would have (I believe) kissed my feet—if I would have allowed it—seemed altogether like a dream after reading the *Arabian Nights*. The novelty of the scene is past, but I shall, I hope, never get used to seeing the wretched creatures treated like beasts of burden, many of them loaded with chains!

We have already made our appearance at the theatre, and I think you would have been amused had you seen Lowry and me playing King and Queen and bowing and curtseying to the sound of drums and trumpets and 'God save the King'! I have since received on one or two evenings, but it would be quite premature to attempt giving any opinion respecting the Society. All I can say is that the first appearance of the French ladies is less pretty and more decorous than I expected. As to our country-women, they are always much the same in this sort of place.

MAURITIUS

You may judge of Lowry's satisfaction when I tell you that immediately upon his arrival he heard that Arthur was expected almost daily."

This expectation was, however, not fulfilled for more than a year.

Lady Frances to Honble. Mrs. Robinson.

August 25th, 1823

"It is impossible to describe how valuable letters are in these distant parts of the world. Since I received your letter on the 22nd, a ship came in bringing a large mail of a few days' later date. My friends have been so kind in writing to me and I received a most delightful packet, the perusal of which made the interest of three or four days. We hear another ship was to leave England for this place the end of May or the beginning of June, by which I hope we shall hear again, as this is the only season in which arrivals are frequent. After November I am told we are not likely to hear for many months, and as this is also the season for hurricanes I think it is probable the communication homewards will not be so frequent as hitherto, so that you must expect a little interval in our correspondence.

Soon after the 20th July we established ourselves here, and you know my tastes well enough to believe I am very glad to find myself once more in the country. This place is the residence of the Commander-in-Chief and at Lowry's disposal, but it is in all respects inferior to Reduit, which we hope to get into better order and which will then be a delightful residence. It is cooler than Port Louis and even at the height of summer is hardly ever unpleasantly hot and the gardens, being extensive and well-shaded, always afford pleasant walks. Hitherto it has been rather cool than otherwise, for the cool season here is always accompanied by a high wind which blows upon you in all directions. I see that much mischief might accrue from neglecting the common precaution recommended in these climates. I never expose myself to the sun—indeed, am very seldom out of the house from eight o'clock in the morning till four in the afternoon. We get up at dawn of day and get a drive, a ride, or a walk before eight o'clock, breakfast half-an-hour afterwards, and I don't stir again till the afternoon. The arrangement suits me very well in all respects, as it gives me a long morning with my children and with this duty my *devoirs de Société* do not much interfere.

This is the season of gaiety and the time when we are expected to contribute to it, but we are only seven miles from Port Louis and I do not find much inconvenience from going in to hold my festivities there. We have already given two great dinners and one great birthday ball on the 12th August. This was on a very large scale and I daresay there were 700 persons present and upwards of 250 at supper at a time, it being the custom here for the ladies to sit down by themselves first and to be succeeded by the gentlemen. We had heard much of the disorder which ensued on these occasions, and Lowry was anxious gently and without giving offence to put it on a more dignified footing. He succeeded in part but not entirely, and I believe the conclusion of the repast was far from decorous.

MAURITIUS

The women really make a great show here. They are generally well-looking without being as handsome as I expected, dress extremely well, and have an air which most Frenchwomen acquire, let them be who they will. Some few, a very few, have had a tolerable education, but the generality are ignorant though inoffensive. How far all the scandal affecting them may be true I cannot pretend to say, but if they are ill-conducted they are not ill-mannered, and I should be disposed to hope are better, in fact, than they have the reputation of being. The men are not by any means prepossessing and they all look like the *demi-soldes*[1] in France.

Hitherto Lowry's administration has gone on very peaceably, although he has had some unpleasant things to do and say by some individuals, but uniting the two commands is a great advantage and taking a straightforward path clear of all party and prejudice a still greater one. And I flatter myself he may find the situation less troublesome than he expected."

The first impression made on the inhabitants by the new Governor and his wife was good, as a letter from a professional gentleman in Mauritius to his brother in Belfast shows:

"We have had great changes and reductions since the arrival of Sir Lowry Cole. He is a most active man and to all appearance a most upright and just one. He is very popular. He has cut off all sinecures and seems determined to be guided by his own observation of characters in the distribution of

[1] Officers retired on half-pay.

his favours. He is too open-hearted and honest an Irishman to listen to intriguers and is always too busily employed to leave himself time to do so. His lady is also a most amiable woman. They have five fine children whom she instructs herself. She is so domestic as to look into her family affairs, even to seeing the bedrooms are in good order and attending to every household affair the same as an English farmer's wife. In doing this, she sets an example that was much needed in this profligate immoral island, and what makes it come with double force is that she is one of the best-informed, clever women of whom England can boast."

The arrival of Arthur Cole at the Mauritius was a great event in the lives of the brothers, who had not seen each other for twenty-five years. Family letters show that in their youthful days there had been a coldness, a want of mutual understanding much regretted by their brothers and sisters. The passing of the years had softened their characters, old unkindnesses were forgotten, and when at last they met at the Mauritius in 1826 they greeted one another with genuine affection and emotion.

Arthur's career had been a very successful one. In 1809, when posted at Mysore as Senior Assistant in charge, a rebellion had broken out in the Maharajah's dominions. He had taken command of his master's troops in the field and defeated the rebels, and by his courage and resource averted a great danger to the State. For this action he got great credit from Lord Minto, the Governor-General. The latter (writing to Mr. Robinson) expressed his praise in very flattering terms as follows:

MAURITIUS

"Mr. Cole has distinguished himself so much in the late important crisis, and the part he has acted on the occasion of the late mutiny and revolt has been so marked and conspicuous, that nothing it is possible to do for him can adequately reward either his merits or his services. He is appointed acting Resident in Mysore . . . and I have assured him that upon a vacancy happening in the Residency the appointment is his of right and, having won it, he shall wear it."

Lady Frances describes to the same "Little Aunt Robinson" her new brother-in-law:

"I think it is since I last wrote to you—February, 1826—that our Indian brother has arrived. I am sorry to say he came in a very weak state of health, but I think he has improved in the last fortnight and his physicians are of opinion that change of climate will entirely set him up. He must have been a magnificent man when in health—six feet three in height and broad in proportion. He has still a very handsome face and pleasing countenance, not like any other of the family but yet bearing a resemblance to two or three of them. *Moralement*, he fully deserves the popularity he has acquired in India, for, besides his intrinsic good qualities, he has a particularly pleasing and attractive manner."

Sir Lowry in a letter to Lord Enniskillen gives a few descriptive lines on the brother who was practically a stranger to all of them:

"He is unlike you and me in one respect, viz. in not being easily irritated or vexed and appears to have an uncommon sweet temper with the most susceptible mind I ever saw, and generosity itself. ... He still looks back with regret at not having gone into the Army. ... In temper you would not believe him to be a Cole. I do not know a sweeter disposition. Our races are just over and he has been very successful with an English half-bred horse I brought with me and gave him on his arrival. I made a course for him at Reduit and it has been an occupation and a very great amusement to him to have the training of his horses. He beats anyone I ever saw in his passion for horses—you are nothing to him."

Sir Lowry's position was, however, not without its difficulties. The offices of military and civil governor were first combined in his person. With this change came others. The new Governor was expected to live with more pomp and ceremony than had previously been done and yet to carry out extensive reforms and economies. Great tact was to be exercised, for the inhabitants disliked the English Government, which had not treated them generously or perhaps even fairly, and had no liking for individual Englishmen, from whom they differed in language, religion and sentiments. One point in favour of the English has never been forgotten, however. When the island was ceded to Great Britain, she undertook not to interfere with the laws or the religion of the inhabitants. This promise has been strictly kept. It is, I am told, still a matter of surprise that it should be so.

The official correspondence with the Colonial Office shows the kindly personal interest Sir Lowry took in the people he ruled over, going into the smallest matter to do them a service. It might be that he knew of a man going to London for the first time on business, who would naturally need a friend to advise him: Sir Lowry furnished him with a suitable introduction. Another wished his son's education as a lawyer completed—what would be the expense at Edinburgh? There were numerous suchlike cases to be investigated and helped. The Governor spared no pains and treated all with the same impartiality, common sense and justice.

In the same spirit he dealt with the larger questions affecting the welfare of the colony's trade, the thorny difficulties of the slave trade and its abolition, and before long the value of his efforts was understood. The planters, who formed the larger proportion of the inhabitants, wanted the same protection for their produce as was enjoyed by the West Indian Islands. Sir Lowry was instrumental in obtaining this boon, in alliance with Sir R. Farquhar, who had been the first British Governor of Mauritius.

The point most strongly impressed on Sir Lowry, namely, that of retrenchment, he found very difficult to carry out according to the views of the Colonial Office. The public buildings had been neglected to the point of ruin; repairs, to be satisfactory, cost more than was considered necessary in London, yet had to be put on a proper footing. Reforms were greatly needed, especially in the public offices, where there was great slackness in the carrying on of business and where many abuses had crept in. The administration of the law was particularly defective.

Sir Lowry was thorough likewise with the Civil Service. If he found a public servant neglecting his duty notoriously, he wanted him removed and a better man put in his place. "It appears", he writes, "that Mr. C., whom I have placed on half-pay, has never done an hour's duty since his appointment—he is, in fact, a hopeless drunkard." Another man, head of an office, left all the business to be transacted by French clerks, and Sir Lowry was inclined to distrust the French race. Of Colonel D. he says: "I should hope, with reference to the opinion I have expressed of Colonel D.'s inefficiency as a civil engineer, that his long services may be duly considered." Of another: "I shall feel it my duty to represent the propriety of his removal. I think I never saw a more inefficient officer in any high situation." He winds up by saying: "Hitherto I have got on very smoothly with the inhabitants as well as the civil and military departments and I hope I shall continue to do so, but it is hard to say how soon one may be in hot water when you have to deal with Frenchmen".

There were, of course, many public servants for whom he had nothing but praise, and whom he promoted. These needed something done for them which only he could do. One of his earliest reforms was to press the English Government to initiate a system of pensions. Many, he told Lord Bathurst, were getting too old for their work, but were not able to retire, having no pension to look to. Others were in bad health, but could not retire for the same reason. He felt the matter should be put forward.

When Sir Lowry's sister-in-law, Lady Catherine

MAURITIUS

Bell, comfortably settled at the Cape, struck a note of warning in her letter of welcome on their arrival at Fort Louis, she prophesied truly. She said he would find little to please and much to torment him among those he governed. There must always be anxieties, difficulties, disappointments, wounds to *amour propre*, unfair criticism in the path of responsibility. Torment is a strong word, yet hardly too strong for the constant friction and thwarting difficulties which were created by Dr. Slater,[1] the first bishop who had been resident in Mauritius. He quarrelled with his clergy, neglected his flock, and set all lawful authority at defiance, being, as he considered himself, under that of the Archbishop of Paris, who was far enough away not to count. His intercourse with Sir Lowry began tolerably well. In a letter to Lord Bathurst (Secretary of State for the Colonies), Sir Lowry says:

"The Bishop and I are on very good terms and we are more likely to continue so by not being too intimate. I can assure your Lordship that I have every disposition to keep on good terms with him as well as to support him in his authority over his clergy, by whom, I fear, he is not much looked up to. I found him in receipt of double the allowance authorised by your Lordship. Besides which, he has 100 dollars a month from the College funds (which they can ill afford) for the superintendence of the religious instruction of the boys. He has likewise 200 dollars a month from the parish of Port

[1] He was a Benedictine, appointed by the Pope, Vicar Apostolic of not only Mauritius and Bourbon, but of Saint Helena, the Cape of Good Hope, Madagascar, the Seychelles, and all Australia, having his seat in Port Louis, and being bishop (*in partibus*) of Ruopa.

Louis for his table and a small farm near the church. But he is always in debt."

They did not continue to be on good terms, however. Cole writes later:

"Dr. Slater publicly accuses the inhabitants of being no better than infidels and to this he attributes every opposition to his will and pleasure. He has, I believe, written home to this effect, and I feel it right to undeceive your Lordship on this subject. I am very far from thinking there is much religion in the colony, but then I never saw much in any Catholic country. But this I can assert, that there is no disposition shown to mock at religion, and I should rather say a general feeling exists of respect to their Church and their clergy when the latter are deserving of consideration. Men brought up as the great majority of the inhabitants have been till lately, without any religious instruction, are not to be brought to a proper sense of religion by high pretensions and meddling interference. But the inhabitants—at least what I have seen of them—show a great desire to have their children instructed in their religious duties, and it is to the rising generation that we must look for great improvement. It would be endless, my Lord, to state all the vexatious interferences of the Vicar Apostolic in family concerns, and although I feel that my opinion cannot be considered unprejudiced by your Lordship, I have no hesitation in stating my conviction that Dr. Slater has done more to injure than promote the progress of religion in the colony. It is not unusual for him on occasions like the present [Easter] to leave the district church without ser-

MAURITIUS

vices, in order that the Curate may increase the numbers of his congregation in the Church of Port Louis, and I leave your Lordship to judge of the effect of such a proceeding upon the inhabitants. Also the churchwardens have to resist his getting possession of the church funds. He is on bad terms with all his clergy and much in debt."

There is much more of this kind, but Lord Bathurst refused to take any notice. He even reprimanded Sir Lowry for having, as Lord Bathurst said, lost his temper with Dr. Slater.

At last the inhabitants sent a deputation to the Archbishop of Paris complaining of the acts of the Vicar Apostolic, with the result that the former sent out an Abbé or two to report. The scandal had even come to the ears of the Pope! Sir Lowry acquainted the Colonial Secretary with these facts, hoping that Dr. Slater would be removed.—The unsatisfactory part of the affair is that there is no *dénouement*.

Slavery and the abolition of the Slave Trade is too large a subject to enter upon fully in the memoirs of a man who, though in a most responsible position, had to carry out the orders of his Government with exactitude and, very often, not at all in the way he thought best. He differed considerably in his opinion of the methods of the enthusiasts in England, though not of course of their wish to abolish the inhuman system; but he thought the process should have been gradual. The registration of the slaves was a means of protecting them, but at the Mauritius the registration had been so carelessly administered that probably a quarter of their number were unregistered. Sir Lowry writes:

"With respect to the registration, Lord Bathurst is perfectly well aware of my opinion of its nullity as it is at present. I will not suppose for a moment that it can enter into the contemplation of Government to set free all the slaves now in the colony whose registration is defective (and I believe a full fourth liable by law to be seized), the greatest part owing to the careless manner the law was first to be attempted to put into execution. But if contrary to my hopes H.M. Government should consider it right to adopt this measure, I pray that the task may be imposed on some other person and not on me, for I feel the injustice would be so great that I could not—whatever refusing might cost me—put it into execution."

Again, to Lord Bathurst:

"With all my anxiety to meet your Lordship's views on all occasions, I have not yet been able to act on your despatch respecting the slave population.

"I have endeavoured to do what I can to enforce the laws in their favour, and I understand that their condition has been very much improved since the arrival of the English here. I had previously to the receipt of your Lordship's letter requested Mr. Foisy, the Government advocate and the best law opinion as well as the coolest head, to revise the *Code noir* and see what might be done towards further improvement. Mr. F. has been ill and I have not been able to get it from him. Your Lordship will not be surprised that I should delay starting a subject of so delicate a nature and so likely to start irritation without any law opinion on which I can place well-grounded confidence.

"The blacks here are generally much less enlightened and of a more stupid race than those in our West Indian Colonies, and the majority of them have been clandestinely imported into this colony not many years back, and, as far as I can judge, are in every way unfit to receive their freedom. For, if left to themselves, they certainly would not work, and I have no hesitation in saying total ruin to the inhabitants would ensue. Your Lordship may be sure I shall do everything I can to ameliorate their condition. It is, however, an unfortunate time to open a question respecting which there is naturally so much feeling, when the colony is smarting under two such severe calamities as the late hurricanes.

"There is likewise another important consideration connected with the subject—I mean the free coloured population. This class of persons is very numerous and many of them are rising into wealth and consequence and have at times shown a desire to assert their consequence. The Malabars are the most respectable of these people, but the free black population are almost invariably idle, dissipated and will never work but from necessity. This applies principally to the small proprietors. . . ."

He speaks even more emphatically in a private letter to Major Colebrooke, one of the Commissioners appointed to inspect the newly acquired colonies:

29th April, 1829

"My decided objection, however, to remain here is the gross injustice (as it appears to me) which will ensue if the penalties of the law are to be enforced against those whose registries were defective under the old registry. No man's property would be safe, and those, or many of them, who are now in affluence would be totally ruined, and nineteen out of twenty of the blacks themselves anything but benefited by the change.

Accustomed as I have been to the miseries of war, I could not remain here in the situation I hold as a mere spectator (as I should be) and witness all the misery which I am convinced would ensue if everything which has been done contrary to law is to be stirred up and acted upon in the colony.

A protector and guardian of slaves would, I have no doubt, do a great deal of good, but I am free to say, as I have said before, that as far as the registration goes I wish what has passed may be forgotten; if not I only hope they will remove me!"

Two Commissioners had been appointed by the British Government to reorganise the newly acquired colonies, the Cape, Ceylon and the Mauritius; they were to report on details of administration and suggest reforms. Their labours began at the Cape and they did not arrive in the Mauritius till 1826. Theirs was an anomalous position which made it very difficult to steer a straight course. In a letter to the Under-Secretary for the Colonies, Mr. R. W. Hay, Sir Lowry gives his opinion of the Commissioners and their works:

MAURITIUS

"You will probably ere this reaches you have received the Commissioners' reports, which I hope may confirm what I have said. I cannot say that I derive much assistance from their labours. I see little of them, though I have endeavoured to show them all the attention in my power, which I believe they are sensible of, but are not disposed to accept from fear of being supposed to be too intimate with me, which I believe originated in the attack made on them in the papers at home for their supposed intimacy with Lord Charles Somerset at the Cape [where he was Governor]. I saw Major Colebrooke in London before I left England and liked what I saw and heard of him much. Mr. Blair appears to be equally likeable. They have had access to everything and cannot, and (to do them justice) do not, I believe, complain of anything being withheld from them, but they are something like the lion's mouth in Venice where everything went in and nothing came out. If I had anything to conceal, this would not be a pleasant state of things, but, although I have little anxiety on this head, I cannot say it is agreeable to be at the mercy of anybody, however honourable, which in truth I really believe they are. . . . I shall be very happy when the Commissioners begin their enquiries into the state of our judicial establishment, which I have ever considered as the only real grievance this colony has to complain of. It is one that is universally felt by all classes and is daily getting worse, as no set of men can be less respected than many of the members of the Bench. The *chicanerie* of the law proceedings is scarce to be believed, and it is harassing and expensive. The colony has been seven years in our possession, and twelve ceded to us, and no one step towards the amelioration of the system has yet taken place. Every information to be afforded by those best calculated to give an opinion on the subject has been sent home, and you have been long in possession of this in your office. . . ."

In 1827 Lord Bathurst had resigned. His successor at the Colonial Office, the Honble. Frederick Robinson, now Lord Goderich, was, as has been seen, a personal friend of Sir Lowry Cole as well as a connexion, through the marriage of Henrietta Cole with Lord Grantham. This no doubt facilitated the accomplishment of Sir Lowry's wish to be transferred to the Cape of Good Hope. Lord Charles Somerset, then Governor, had resigned and was going home. As a governorship, the Cape was far less good than it had been, the salary having been reduced to £7000 and the country residence formerly occupied by the Governor sold and not replaced by another.

The reforms, the work of the Commissioners, and the difficult problem of the slaves were agitating the minds of the Dutch population so that the prospect for the Governor was not particularly inviting, but Sir Lowry had decided it was best to leave the Mauritius and he had excellent reasons. He would have preferred to go back to England, but he was determined to save for his family, which he was more likely to do abroad. His children were growing too old for the tropics and a change of climate was necessary for the sake of their health. Nevertheless he was sorry to leave the Mauritius. His relations with the inhabitants had been of the

MAURITIUS

happiest during the five years he spent among them and he knew he had given them satisfaction. For many of them he had a great respect and liking and he felt he had been of service to them.

An unfortunate incident occurred just before his departure which gave him great pain, the more so as he felt it might have been averted by the exercise of forethought on his own part. Though now belonging to the British Empire, the inhabitants were French by extraction and French in sentiment. Their great Emperor, his imprisonment at St. Helena, and, as they believed, the cruel treatment of him by his gaoler, Sir Hudson Lowe, were fresh in their memories. It is no wonder, therefore, that when Lowe touched at Port Louis on his way from Ceylon, where he was Governor, to the Cape, their hatred showed itself in an unseemly way.

To Honble. E. G. Stanley.

"SIR, *12th May*, 1828

As you may probably hear an exaggerated account of a very disgraceful proceeding which took place in Port Louis towards Major-General Sir Hudson Lowe on the 1st instant, I think it right to put you in possession of the following facts for the information of Mr. Huskisson.

On the 29th last month, Sir Hudson Lowe touched here in the ship *Alexander* on his passage from Ceylon to England, and being myself aware of the political sentiments of many of the inhabitants of this island regarding the memory of Bonaparte, I mentioned the same to Sir Hudson in order that he might be on his guard.

Sir Hudson Lowe walked about the town of St. Louis with one of my A.D.C.'s on the day of his arrival, but, although his presence created an apparent and not unnatural curiosity on the part of the inhabitants, they did not show any desire to insult him. He afterwards dined with me at the Mess of the 82nd Regiment and the next day drove and rode about the country with his A.D.C. without the slightest appearance of any intent to insult him.

But I am sorry to add that on his way from the Government House in Port Louis to the quay in order to embark, he was assailed by a mob, headed and instigated by persons connected with some of the most respectable families in the colony, who heaped upon him the most abusive and insulting epithets which the French language affords—in allusion to his public conduct at St. Helena. But no violence that I can ascertain was offered to his person. I felt it impossible to pass over in silence such an illiberal outrage and I therefore published a government order of which the enclosed is a copy. Such of the offenders as can be sworn to I intend to proceed against before the Colonial Courts, though I fear it will be difficult to obtain a sentence against them. And those amongst the instigators and abettors who are foreigners (Frenchmen residing here on sufferance only) I propose to order them to quit the colony. But I shall have the honour of writing further on this subject and to have to transmit to you the decision, whatever it may be, of the Colonial Courts.

I have the honour, etc.,
Your obed^t. Servant,
G. Lowry Cole"

MAURITIUS

The incident had no further consequences at the time, and the steps taken by Sir Lowry to show the offenders the error of their ways were successful, for they presented many apologetic petitions profusely signed—there is a quarto volume of these—till even their Governor's wrath was appeased. But it made him realise how slender were the ties which bound the inhabitants to Great Britain and how easily they might be broken. He did not think the Colonial Office was sufficiently aware of this danger and he tried to open Lord Goderich's eyes. This letter, which he wrote from the Cape in 1832, shows that his fears were still awake, and his interest in the island as keen as ever. It shows also that whatever his feelings about the French in general might be, he resented fiercely the importation of an Englishman to fill a post on which a Frenchman of the island had strong claims.

To Lord Goderich.

CAPE TOWN
25th July, 1832

"MY DEAR LORD,
    ... It would not be right from a false delicacy to withhold from you the knowledge I possess of the actual state of the colony and of the feeling and temper of the parties received from persons on whose judgment and veracity I can place implicit confidence and who from the situation they hold ought and must know what is going on.
    This excitement was not unforeseen by me when I heard of Mr. Jeremie's arrival in Table Bay on his way to the Mauritius to fill the situation of Procureur General. . . . I stated to him that if it

was the determination of H.M.'s Government to carry through the measure I understood from him they intended to do, I regretted that he was not accompanied by a sufficient armed force to preclude any attempt on the part of the inhabitants to resist them by force of arms.

It is not my wish or intention to make any observations on the line of conduct adopted by my friend Sir Charles Colville.[1] From a residence of five years there, no one is more sensible than I am of the difficulties he has had to contend with. The Mauritius, as you know, is in many respects very unlike the West Indian Islands. In the former the proprietors are resident and managers of their own property and the proportion between the slave and the white and free population does not exceed four to one, if so much. The white part and a great part of the coloured are generally armed and are accustomed to the use of arms for their amusement, and they are, I am satisfied, fully equal to keep the slave population in restraint without assistance from the troops, and the natural restlessness and intemperance of Frenchmen is increased in them by a tropical climate. They are not deficient in moral courage or in intellectual qualities. Many of them possess very considerable ability as well as ambition, but without judgment or discretion to guide them. They appear to have gone too far for them to recede and one cannot well see how they can end without bloodshed—or by the departure of Mr. Jeremie, a circumstance I do not wish to foresee, although I must in candour say I most sincerely regret he was ever sent there, as in my opinion a

[1] He succeeded Cole at the Mauritius.

more obnoxious person could not have been fixed upon. Besides which he superseded the most popular, influential, able and respected man at the Bar and the only reasonable man of any weight at all.

Regarding the above-mentioned Monsieur d'Épinay, I had an opportunity of hearing from himself, when he touched here on his return journey to the Mauritius from his trip to England and France, how much changed his political sentiments and feelings were, and I really believe he was very well affected to our Government at that time; but I will not now say (notwithstanding my good opinion of him) what effect his removal in the way it has been done may have had upon him, for he possesses a good share of vanity and is not insensible to his own talents and his position of influence in the colony. When it was considered advisable at home to send out an Englishman and a stranger as Procureur General, it is, I think, to be regretted that the situation of third Judge of Appeal with a good salary was not offered to Monsieur d'Épinay.

The newspaper reports the appointment of General Nicolay to succeed Sir Charles Colville, who, it is said, has been recalled. I sincerely hope, my dear Lord, this report is without foundation. General Nicolay is not known as a public man in any way except perhaps in your office or (what is more to the purpose) at the Anti-Slavery Society as a West Indian Governor who has given satisfaction as such. In the present state of the Mauritius this will only add fuel to the flame already raised by Mr. Jeremie's arrival, and I should really apprehend the consequences, without General Nicolay is accompanied by a considerable additional force."

Cole goes on to say that the garrison of three regiments should be increased to six, besides a considerable naval force, and that the defences already decided upon should be pushed on to completion. He gives a passing word of the expense of all this and adds that if a war with France breaks out, the certainty of the loss of the islands will follow, unless a more conciliatory system is adopted.

"I will not deny that, notwithstanding the very inexcusable faults and absurdities of the inhabitants I entertain a strong feeling of regard for many of them and shall ever take a kindly interest in the affairs of the colony. I spent five very happy years there and should like to prevent if possible its total destruction and preserve it to the British Empire as a place of considerable importance so long as we possess India."

CHAPTER XIV

AT THE CAPE OF GOOD HOPE

IN 1813, when Napoleon's power was obviously waning, the Netherlands was among the first to break away. Its Government welcomed back the Prince of Orange, who had passed his exile either in England or serving in Spain with the English army. In 1814 the English Government, which had been holding the Cape Colony by right of conquest since 1806, wished for a sounder claim. They made an agreement with the sovereign prince of the Netherlands to buy it for the sum of six million pounds sterling, which included certain Dutch provinces in South America. The Convention was signed in London in August 1814.

Though this agreement had extinguished the hopes of the Dutch of ever belonging to Holland again, they were not discontented. Few if any important changes had been made, their language was still used in the public offices and their religion and Church protected. But this state of things was not likely to continue as the Colony began to interest English people and the Government hoped to find in immigration a way out of the many difficulties left by more than twenty years' war. Parliament voted £50,000 to defray the cost of sending out a large party to the Cape. Many thousands sent in their names, and from them a selection was made. Some were people of certain means who brought with them servants and apprentices; there were artisans, factory hands, clerks and storemen. As may be supposed a large proportion knew little about farming and for some years suffered a good deal of distress. Eventually the artisans, dispersing through the villages, got plenty of work, so that both the Dutch farmers and the English settlers were benefited.

But Cape Colony was no longer exclusively Dutch. The first change, and one that embittered the old colonists, was an order of the home Government that after January 1st, 1825, all official documents, and after January 1st, 1828, all proceedings in Courts of Law, should be in English. Another very great grievance was the reduction in the value of the paper money, about a third of which had been created by the English Government; a seventh of the remainder were clever forgeries and the rest of Dutch origin. Though it was necessary to do this for the sake of commerce, it came as a crushing blow to many people and many were ruined.

Government schools were started to which the inhabitants were invited to send their children free, but as the teaching was in English even in the western part of the country, where Dutch was spoken, this was resented.

Another innovation, which, however, probably did not annoy the Boers, was the institution of a Council to advise the Governor in affairs of importance which consisted of six officials nominated by the Secretary of State. This was one of the reforms inaugurated by the two Commissioners already referred to. Lord Charles Somerset, who was Governor at this time, paid but little attention to the advice of his Council and was very arbitrary in his methods and in his treatment of anyone who opposed him. So many complaints of his tyranny were made to the Colonial Secretary that he found it necessary to return to England.

Having made a good deal of interest to obtain the post of Governor at the Cape, Sir Lowry could not very well refuse it, though late events had disillusioned him considerably as to the prospects, and he realised that, except in the matter of climate, the change would not be for the better: but for the benefit of his family that exception was of the utmost importance. He sums up the pros and cons in a letter to a friend who was at that time Chancellor of the Exchequer:

To the Right Honble. Henry Goulburn.

June 16*th*, 1828
REDUIT, Mauritius
"MY DEAR GOULBURN,
From the numerous changes which have taken place during the last twelve months in the Ministry at home, it is difficult at this distance to guess who will be in when this reaches you. But I see by our last papers that my friend Goderich is out and that you are Chancellor of the Exchequer. . . .

Of my acceptance of an appointment to the Cape Government you must know of course—and although well considered at the time, from what I have since learned of affairs there, I doubt whether it would not have been wiser for me to have obtained permission to have gone home at the end of the year on leave. To remain here with my family another hot summer would not have been advisable.

Between Lord Charles Somerset and Sir Rufam Donkin's squabbles, and the Commissioner's reforms and I might say upsetting of every old institution there, with a very diminished income and a country house to be provided out of it, I am not sanguine enough to look forward to derive either credit or profit by my residence there; it will probably therefore not be very long.

>I am, yours sincerely,
>G. L. COLE"

The new Governor of Cape Colony with his wife and children—now numbering seven—arrived in the spring of 1828. It must have been a relief to leave the Mauritius, its hot climate, the infrequent communication with home—for there were months when no letters came—for the Cape of Good Hope. There the climate was excellent, the distance to England was shorter and there was a variety of society, since all the ships passing to and from India and China stopped in Table Bay. Also Lady Frances had the pleasure of the company of her sister, Lady Catherine, whose husband, Colonel Bell, was Colonial Secretary. The officials were for the most part English, whereas in the Mauritius the larger proportion were French Creoles.

The following extract from the journal of an American tourist describes their *entourage:*

"The next evening I was engaged to dine at the cottage of Governor Cole, ten miles in the country, with Captain Finch, Dr. Malone, and Captain Bruce.

"At half-past six we took our seats in a Landau

and in little more than an hour found ourselves whirling through the gates of Protea, the name given by Sir Lowry to the estate from the abundance of Silver-tree surrounding it. The former country seat of the Governor of the Colony, the Newlands, in the same vicinity, was a splendid establishment costing the British Government, it is said, during the administration of Lord Charles Somerset, the predecessor of General Cole, £80,000; but this had been sold and Protea is the private property of the Governor, upon which improvements are but just commencing, it having been in his possession only a short time. It seemed an unpretending establishment for a Captain General.

"We had been apprised that it was but a family party we were to join; and on entering the drawing-room found just the circle that those long cut off from the enjoyment of refined and polished society would wish to meet, divested of everything like the formality and etiquette of an entertainment of state.

"Lady Frances with two or three female companions and four lovely daughters from 5 to 12 years of age; the Governor and his Aide-de-Camps military and civil; the Attorney-General and lady, the Surgeon of the household and one or two young officers in the uniform of the Scotch regiments constituted the numbers. The General in the full uniform of his rank, scarlet with epaulets and cordons of gold, received us in the centre of the room and after an interchange of salutations presented each of our company in order to his lady and then to the party in general.

"Nothing in a family circle has a greater charm

for me than a group of well-managed and lovely children and the daughters of the household in a uniform of scarlet crêpe with blue ribbons on their necks to match their bright eyes attracted my first attention. The two younger quickly threw off the reserve imposed by the entrance of strangers, while every look and every action told they had been trained by no inferior hand—by their vivacity and playfulness presented a delightful picture of happiness; and it was with sincere regret that I perceived the whole number when dinner was announced kissing goodnight to Lady Frances as she gave her hand to Captain Finch to be led to the *salle à manger*.

"The entertainment in the dining-room was all that elegance and taste could desire. On rejoining the ladies at ten o'clock for a cup of tea, I was gratified with a richer enjoyment in addition to the conversation taking place—in the privilege of looking over a sketch-book of Lady Cole filled with drawings from nature manifesting a high degree of native and cultivated talent.

"Both Lady Frances and her sister Lady Catherine Bell are distinguished for their high mental endowments and for their various accomplishments and I was happy to learn that the influence of their rank and talents in the Colony is cast in favour of rational enjoyments and of piety. Lady Frances is not only the Patroness but a Superintendent of a Sabbath School in the Episcopal Church.

"The General and his family take possession of the Government House in Cape Town in a few days for the winter and on the 23rd inst. a great

Fête in honour of the birthday of his Britannic Majesty is to be given by them. Invitations were early issued to the officers of our ship and both the General and his Lady expressed a cordial wish before taking leave of us that we might remain for this entertainment."

In the autumn of 1829 Sir Lowry made himself acquainted with the Colony under his charge from end to end, travelling partly on horseback and partly in the roomy wagon of the country; sometimes camping out but more often enjoying the hospitality of various officials in the towns and villages. His party consisted of his A.D.C., Baron During, and another Secretary, accompanied usually by the Commissioner of the District and two or three servants.

Letters to his wife relate his experiences:

"MY DEAREST LOVE,
　　　A thousand thanks for your letter of yesterday. . . .
The Broede River, which is half an hour from this, is so full that we were obliged to cross in a small punt and merely take what we wanted for the night and leave the waggon and baggage and servants at the other side. We got them over this morning, but were obliged to take everything out of the waggons and get empty casks under them and tow them over by bullocks. . . .
The wind was so high that there was no inducement to ride and we had the waggons close-buttoned up to keep it out.
The scenery is much like you have seen with less

cultivation and trees, but the width of the valley greater.

We shall get into the Karroo tomorrow evening and until I reach Beaufort or Graaff Reynett I shall not have an opportunity of writing to you.

Adieu my love.

Ever your attached and affec^te,

G. L. C."

Graff Reynett
17th Sept., 1829

"We start today on our way to Somerset. The journey through the Karroo to Beauford was fagging and dreary. There is certainly nothing very seductive in the Karroo. If there was wood and water it would be very fine, but there is really scarce a green shrub, much less a tree to be seen, and the road in many places terrible. Strong as our waggons are it does astonish me how we got through without an accident.

The water, which is very scarce, is not so bad as it has been represented to be. At least we continue to drink it in tea and otherwise. We saw few wild animals. None of the larger kind except Spring Buck of which we saw some thousands, between this and Beauford. The crops which are only here and there in patches where the Farmer can irrigate, are looking well and the people appear to be in better spirits, but they complain sadly of the Hottentots and Bushmen. The latter have committed several murders and have carried off a great many cattle from the Farmers on the Frontier.

This place is like fairy scenery after what we have seen, the streets shaded with lemon trees and the

AT THE CAPE OF GOOD HOPE

houses clean and nice, the hedges and gardens as green as you would see them anywhere.

We halted here yesterday, but it was not a day of rest to me as I had to visit everything and hold a Levee to receive petitions and compliments from the Boers and Inhabitants and a dinner of 16 or 18 afterwards.

My letters from Stockenstroem are very satisfactory on the state of things there and although the Caffirs are stealing cattle every night, it does not appear that they have any idea of invading (as was supposed by Colonel Somerset) the Colony.

Tell my Popsy that I have got an ostrich egg for her which I took out of the nest myself, having seen the Mama get off it. There were 21 eggs in the nest. We have seen few bulbs and Brown has not been able to get you many."

GRAHAMSTOWN, 25*th Sept.*, 1829

"Upon the whole I have found my tour much less fatiguing than I had expected and with fewer inconveniences. I rode the greatest part of the way.

The Farmers have suffered dreadfully from Locusts and drought in the district. One of the name of Cotze lost 2800 sheep, 450 oxen and 45 horses and he and his brother where we slept one night are reduced to buy on credit grain and potatoes for seed. The latter has as nice a farm with clipped hedges as you would see anywhere. I have not met with so much industry since I have been in the Colony. He has built a very good house and as he says, and I believe with truth, there is not as much straw in the district as would thatch it!

His crops look well at present and the springs

which were dried up last year are now running, and if no new misfortunes occur he may recover a little this year. The situation of his farm is rather pretty, but there is not much beauty in the country until you arrive at Somerset at the back of which the mountains are picturesque with some coppice woods in the little glens.

The village is quite in its infancy and like all the new villages in this country very straggly—the public Buildings with very few exceptions being ill-built and quite out of repair.

The open part of the country for some distance about Somerset is very like Wiltshire with less appearance of verdure. There was running water in the little Fish River, which was a novelty. The country between Grahamstown and Somerset is rugged and was entirely covered with brushwood, but few or no heaths.

The Fish River, which we on horseback crossed several times, is not visible until you are quite over the banks and is scarcely passable even for a horse or cattle except at the fords—from the abruptness and height of the banks.

This is a large place, but very straggling and I suspect will remain so for years; with a very large commodious Church without taste in the centre of the main street, scarce such a thing as a tolerable house, generally thatched and not unlike houses you see in an Irish village. The Drostdy [Town-hall] House looking down the principal street quite in a ruinous state, two stories high without a tree about it. Colonel Somerset's house which is seen from the town is rather pretty and may be made very much so. I breakfasted with him there yesterday and found what I saw of the house very comfortable. She has been a handsome woman, at least what is generally considered so by the world, rather stiff in her manner. They must I conceive lead a very dull life as they appear not to be on visiting terms with any of the principal people here, at which I am surprised as the civil officers here are really very well informed and agreeable judging by the little I have seen of them. . . ."

Oct. 9th

"I have been to my tour of the Frontier and have seen half of the Chiefs and am to see the remaining half to-day. It is very much to be regretted that they were ever permitted to cross the Frontier, but without going too far with them we cannot well drive them over it. I hope the visit may have done some good."

GRAHAMSTOWN, 20*th Oct.* 1829

"During accompanied me as far as Stockenstroem's farm, at the Kaka where I left him to shoot birds for your Ladyship, as it was inconvenient to take more people with me than was necessary. I reached Cradock in a little more than eight hours accompanied by Captain Campbell and Stockenstroem. We were received with a great appearance of pleasure by the Inhabitants, who had never had the honour of a Governor's visit before.

I slept at the Minister's, Mr. Taylor, a Scotchman who gave us one dish which he called a roast lamb entire, but which should with more propriety have been called a sheep.

The next day we started early with the intention

of visiting the Scotch settlement on the Bavians River, now called Glen Linden, to get the inhabitants to agree about the situation of a new Church, but we had not left more than half an hour when we encountered as severe a storm of Hail and Rain accompanied by thunder as I was ever out in. I really do not exaggerate in saying the hailstones were considerably larger than musket-balls. I am sure we did not see less than from twenty to thirty of the Farmer's flock lying dead or dying along the road.

The river was so up that it was considered impossible to reach the Kaka that night. We stopped for the night about four hours short of it where we were well received, but not very well accommodated, but the poor people did their best which is all one could ask for.

We sent a man to the junction of the Bavians and Great Fish River to let us know if the ford was passable the next morning. He did not arrive until ten o'clock, stating it to be so. We set off as soon as we could and after a ride of five hours reached the ford and found that the report was not correct and the river not fordable—to our no small annoyance having brought nothing with us.

There are few or no habitations on the left bank of the river. We had, therefore, to look our for some place for the night where we could get something to eat as well as shelter. After about three-quarters of an hour we found the location of a Boer and his family who go under the denomination of a Squatter. He had luckily erected a wooden hut, one end of which he gave up to us, but had nothing but meal and milk and eggs to offer us. The water was too thick to drink and having no vegetables or any substitute for bread we had a very uncomfortable meal, and a still more uncomfortable lodging as no one was provided with a mattress but myself and the beds and skins my three companions slept on were offensive to a very great degree. I do not recollect having ever passed a more uncomfortable evening or night."

"My dearest Love,   Uitenhage, 28*th Oct.* 1829

I am now about a hundred miles nearer to you than I have been for some time and as the distance diminishes I get more anxious for its termination and begin to count the days. The three last days' travelling were rather severe, and I am not sorry for a halt here today and tomorrow.

My companions are dropping off one by one. Dickenson appears to stand the journey best, the Baron looks very old, as I do myself; but he is older in habits than I am and is slower and more methodical than ever and not very useful on a journey.

This place is well situated, the best of any district town I have seen with the exception of Graff Reynett. It is very well watered which in Cape-land is everything and will in the course of time most probably be a considerable town—at present like all new places the houses much scattered, but less so than Grahamstown over which it has many advantages. Stockenstroem is to have his headquarters here. I dined with him yesterday. The society does not appear to me so good as at Grahamstown.

I go tomorrow to Algoa Bay and the day following I turn my head towards my old woman where I need not say my heart is already. You will find me sadly burnt and old-looking. However I am very well in health and better able to undergo fatigue than when I left you. The Baron gets older and older except when he sees a fern which is new to him. Dickenson is quite fresh and undergoes the fatigue particularly well and eats for two at all times of the day."

Georgi, Monday morning
November 9th

"We arrived here yesterday evening after a rather fagging ride, having to ride along some of the coast as the mouth of one of the rivers was closed by sand and the waters up in consequence. It was severe work for the horses as well as riders—and to my very great annoyance I found they had prepared a public dinner in the house I am to put up in. This you may suppose did not put me in a very good humour. However nothing could have been more discreet and quiet than they were and I got to bed, as they left the house when I got up from table."

It was part of his plan that Lady Frances with some of the children should meet him on his way back, and the letters are full of directions for this operation. Plainly, the object was to show her the new road over the Pass to Hottentots' Holland and Caledon which had just been made under his direction and which still bears his name—"Sir Lowry's Pass".[1]

This had been undertaken without authorisation from home and his expenditure brought censure

---

[1] "Colesberg" also keeps the memory of his rule.

upon him, as will be seen from the following letter to his friend Lord Goderich:

CAPE TOWN
4th April, 1831

"MY DEAR LORD,

Rest assured that I shall attend strictly to your caution on the subject of expense which however it is difficult to do in a Colony where every public building has been either a job or let to fall into ruin.

I may say in confidence to you that Lord Charles [Somerset] has done more injury to the Colony in this and many other respects than half a century will recover.

Look at the Commissioner's report of Government House in Cape Town which they considered so bad as to recommend a new one should be built for the Governor . . . . If I cannot justify myself for the expense incurred in repairs and alterations made in Government House in Cape Town, let me be surcharged with it, but I cannot but feel it unjust for my successor, whoever he may be, that he should be deprived by my fault from what I consider to be absolutely necessary for his health and comfort.

As to the allowance which was promised for a country house, I feel convinced that you will, if you can with propriety, restore it to me, but I am well aware that in these times of general outcry against expense you may find it impossible to do so.

As relates to the expense incurred by me on the new pass over the mountain at Hottentots' Holland, I am free to confess as I have stated in my despatch that I deserved censure for not previously asking permission to do so. Having however convinced my own mind of its public utility, and ascertained by personal inspection its practicability at an expense I considered inconsiderable, as regards its public advantages, I cannot, however I may wince at the censure I received, regret having taken this step. The Colonists are sensible of its utility and are grateful for the benefit they have already derived from it. But however advantageous a work may be, you may rest assured that I shall not readily subject myself to a similar reproof in future.

I will venture to assert that no Governor takes more pains to keep down expense than I have done, but I am very far from thinking it Economy to permit public buildings to fall into ruin, which is very much the case in this country.

The Colony, as you must be aware, is miserably poor with a semi-barbarous population scattered over an immense tract of bad land, separated from the more civilised parts by mountains over which there are few passes and those of a description that would not be considered passable for a wheel carriage in any other country in the world, I believe.

Being cut off from a market for their produce, there is no stimulus for industry, and the Inhabitants must ever remain in their present state of poverty and semi-barbarism until these passes are made passable. This can only be done by Government as there is no Capital. And if there was, it could never pay as a speculation. And I know of no measure which would give so much general satisfaction or tend to make the inhabitants English or would forward the views of Government as regards the Abolition of Slavery so much as an authorised progressive system for the improve-

ment of these barriers against Industry and Civilization.
   Most sincerely and affec^(ately) yours,
                              G. LOWRY COLE"

Again in a letter of September 18th, 1831:

"Make what reductions you please. I doubt whether the Colony will for many years be able to pay the Cape Corps, although the Eastern Frontier trade with the Caffirs and the interior of the Continent is rapidly increasing. The wine trade has, I fear, seen its best days and is on the decline, and corn and hides are at present the only things to look up to.
"The tax you propose on Slaves would only accelerate the ruin of the wine-growers for they are the principal slave owners, and without a favourable answer to my representation on the Slave Ordinance I do not think it would be advisable to increase the discontent which already exists to a very considerable degree against the British Government by laying on a tax on Slaves."

Sir Lowry had obtained permission to go home on leave in 1832, and as he had not resigned his post no one was appointed to replace him. But the subordinate in whose hands the government of the Colony would be left was not, he thought, suitable or capable of ruling under such difficult circumstances, and accordingly he writes to Lord Goderich on March 11th, 1832:

"I am persuaded things would not long go on

well or satisfactorily to either your Lordship or the Colony. You are aware from my private and public letters of the irritation which the Slave Ordinance has created here in the minds of the inhabitants generally and you are likewise in possession of my opinion upon the late Schedule of Reduction and of the probable effects in the Colony, and the state of excitement and dissatisfaction which exists among the Boers on the Eastern Frontier—and the causes thereof. Although far from apprehending any very serious disturbance to result therefrom, at the same time, with a knowledge of the revolutionary feelings which exist everywhere at home, it would be presumption in me to assert that none can be apprehended ... and thinking so I should ill require or deserve your friendship were I for my own personal convenience or advantage to avail myself of the leave you have so kindly granted. It is, I confess, a very great disappointment ... I am heartily tired of a situation where I feel I can do but little good and where I can see no favourable alteration of circumstances.

I only look forward to a Successor to arrive in January next year."

Cole had had proof of the irritation caused by the new Slave regulations. In 1830 the quantity and quality of food to be given to the slaves was prescribed, their clothing, hours of work and many other details regulated in a way which the owners declared destroyed their authority. Excitement in Cape Town became so great that the Governor found it necessary to prohibit public meetings and to threaten to punish anyone who disturbed the peace.

AT THE CAPE OF GOOD HOPE

When things became quieter he consented to a public meeting being held, and about two thousand slave-owners came together in Cape Town. The utmost order was maintained, though resolutions were carried protesting against the new laws. The whole assembly then marched to the open space in front of Government House and two gentlemen were deputed to inform the Governor that the slave holders were prepared to suffer the penalties of the orders in Council, but could not obey them.

Finally, in 1833, an Emancipation Act came into force in all British possessions by which, after a short term of apprenticeship, negroes were to have the same civil rights as white people.

The sum of twenty million pounds sterling was voted in Parliament to be divided among the various colonies as compensation for the value of the slaves, which it was thought would be sufficient; but when in 1835 the share awarded to the Cape was found to be a little less than one million and a quarter, a panic was created.

The money of all sorts of people was invested in slaves. In some cases they had been the sole property of widows or minors or aged people who were now reduced to indigence.

The worst of all these bad arrangements of the Government was their refusal to send the money out to South Africa, and that each claim must be proved before the Commissioners in London, when the amount would be paid in stock after certain charges were deducted. Numbers of agents came into existence who bought up the claims at much less than their real value. It is easy to realise the misery and poverty that resulted.

Sir Lowry left the Colony in 1833 and was spared seeing the ruin which he could not have mitigated. His successor was Sir Benjamin D'Urban.

During the four years of Sir Lowry's rule, the Kaffirs were tolerably peaceful and it was not necessary to send an armed expedition against them. With the help and advice of Sir J. Stockenstrom, a Dutchman, of whom he had a very high opinion, Sir Lowry made an experiment for their benefit. There was some land which had been ceded to the Colony by one of the native chiefs, Gaika by name, on the Kat river, where there were well-watered valleys and fertile lands suitable for farming. Between two and three thousand Hottentots were settled in small holdings and supplied with seed corn and other necessaries for cultivating their land. The settlers were to remain five years, at the end of which time those who had built themselves cottages and tilled the land were to receive grants in freehold. The holdings of the unsuccessful were to revert to Government. It was found that the pure Hottentots could not endure a regular life, but some of the half-breeds did and settled down well.

By the autumn of 1832, Sir Lowry was in sight of the end, and on September 18th he wrote to his brother, Lord Enniskillen, to condole with him on a bereavement. "The poor Granthams" had also suffered misfortunes, and all this stimulated his desire to retire; and he had written asking either for leave of absence or for recall; his hope was to sail in February when the home-bound Indian and China ships touched at the Cape, as it was hard to get accommodation for a large family in any smaller vessel.

"As the time approaches I am getting more anxious to return to those from whom in heart and affection I have never been absent. Although the state of affairs at home is not very inviting to me with so large and so young a Family as mine. But I feel we are all growing old and I have lost so many of my family in the last few months that I wish if possible to embrace once more those who are still left me and enjoy so much of their society in this world as the Almighty may be pleased to grant me.

"My elder children are of an age to require better instruction than this place can afford, and independent of these reasons—with the exception of a very fine climate and the gratification it is to Fanny to have her sister with her—I have no inducement to remain here. In fact I am tired of being a Governor and shall be too happy to descend to the humbler walks of life. All I wish at present is to give my children a good education and principles before I die. I hope they have the principles, but am a good deal disappointed in the expectation I had formed from the report of others of any of them turning out scholars. I believe the fact to be that they have too much of the Cole in them to be fond of learning. It is to be hoped they may have their good qualities if they have their defects.

"I cannot say how it gratifies me to hear so good an account of Cole [Lord Enniskillen's son]. The manner he has been returned for the County must be very flattering to you. I was glad to hear he likes home—Ireland never wanted resident proprietors more than she appears to do at present. I cannot but feel that the Reform Bill is a very ticklish experiment. I see it has been carried by a great majority in the Commons, and although I do not like the idea that the Lords should be bullied into a measure they disapprove of, it would appear by the papers that so much excitement has been created in favour of the Bill among people in general that it is impossible at this distance not to feel some apprehensions of the result if it is thrown out by the Lords. God grant it may all end well! ... When we meet, which God grant we may soon, you will find me grown old in every way.

"My children promise to be very tall, but I hope not *quite* so tall as yours. They are what may be called well-looking. Pop [his eldest girl] has lost her good looks very much. Lou [the second] if she had not red hair is like her Aunt Florence [Balfour]. The two youngest girls healthy little things, the youngest quite a Cole, and the other her mother in miniature. I think I have given you a dose of it, so Adieu.

Your affec^te and attached Brother,
G. L. COLE."

So ends the public life of a famous soldier who had proved himself also a shrewd, conscientious and capable colonial administrator.

After his return to England in 1833, Sir Lowry lived at Highfield Park, near Hartford Bridge in Hampshire. He had been promoted to the full rank of General in 1830 during his absence at the Cape.

AT THE CAPE OF GOOD HOPE

Four years earlier, when the death of the Marquess of Hastings (better known as Lord Moira) left the colonelcy of the Inniskilling Fusiliers vacant, Lowry Cole was appointed Colonel of the regiment with which so many associations linked him. Six of the battle honours inscribed on the banner of the 27th Foot, from Maida to Orthez, had been won under his command. It was in all ways fitting that when he died suddenly in 1842, in his seventy-first year, his remains should be conveyed with full military honours to Enniskillen for burial in the family vault; and that at Enniskillen he should be commemorated by a lofty column on which stands his statue in full military array.

APPENDIX A

Extract from a letter dated Bandon, 6th Jany., from Captain Robert Crawford, R. F. Artillery, to Colonel Lowry Cole

THE first appearance of the French fleet off Bantry Bay was on the 22nd Dec.; the same evening General Dalrymple received an express to that effect.

On the 23rd the alarm became general and Captain Lunt Carr was sent forward to Bandon with four six-pounders.

On Saturday, the 24th, a number of artillery-men were brought from Cork harbour to man the field pieces.

We were ready on Sunday night and anxious to meet the enemy, but waited for orders till Wednesday, when an order was received to send 40 artillery-men back to Cork harbour, which was directed to Lt. Colonel Arabin at Bandon,[1] with two $5\frac{1}{2}$-inch Howitzers—all we could man.

I accompanied him. We have waited there since for orders.

Having thus far informed you of our departments, I shall strive to give you an accurate account of movements in and near Bandon.

On the evening of the 23rd, the Wexford Militia and a troop of Lord Jocelyn's Dragoons quartered in this town moved forward to Dunmanway and were replaced by the Waterford Regiment, the Roscommon and Galway flank companies, the light company of the Caithness Legion, and four six-pounders, under command of Captain Lunt Carr. . . .

3rd Jany. In consequence of an express from General

[1] On which he [apparently Dalrymple] applied to General Stewart and obtained leave to go to Bandon.

Smith that a French fleet was in the Shannon the Sligo Militia marched to Cork, the cavalry to Mallow, and three companies of the Wexford returned here.

I shall now return to the Fleet part. . . .

24th Decr. Seventeen ships of war (most of them of the Line) endeavoured to get into the Bay, which contrary winds prevented. Twenty-five more ships in the offing. The wind still contrary and blowing hard. On Monday a heavy gale from the same point, which continued to increase until Tuesday night when it blew a violent storm, owing to which they were forced out to sea.

29th and 30th part of them returned much shattered and some of them, it was said, had perished in the storm.

31st. I went to Bantry Bay by desire of [1] and Colonel Arabin to reconnoitre the Fleet and country. And on my way I met Generals Dalrymple and Coote on their return from that town, whither they had gone on the 25th, who ordered that I should report to them at Dunmanway on my return, which I gave in as follows, and same night brought to Bandon.

Eight sail of ships, two of which were of the Line. Five Frigates and a Lugger lay at anchor inside of the Bay not far from the town. While observing the Fleet I observed a boat full of men (I suppose 40 or 50) board an American Brig and then row near the shore. Upon a party of the Galway Militia under the command of Colonel Finch appearing on the beach, they returned to their ships.

1st, 2nd, 3rd, 4th Jany., the ships continued near Bantry, but the weather being hazy it was difficult to ascertain what their force was off the Bay. This occasioned a variety of reports here, many of which, though coming by express, were contradictory.

5th. They weighed anchor and put to sea, leaving behind them two vessels that appeared disabled, which followed them this morning and could not be discerned from shore when the express left Bantry.

The inclemency of the weather, while it frustrated the

[1] Blank in MS.

APPENDIX A

designs of the enemy, was hard upon our troops, but they endured every fatigue like veterans, and were essentially benefited by the zeal and loyalty of our yeomanry and by the hospitality and humanity of all our countrymen.

I beg you will assure his Lordship that should I have omitted anything material it is not through want of inclination but wholly owing to want of recollection which the confusion attending such occurrences naturally occasions.

APPENDIX B

Instructions for the Honble. Lt. Colonel Cole

Troops	Off.	R. and F.
5th Dragoons	1	30
Kells Yeomanry	2	32
Cork City Militia	5	200
Total	8	262

and a light 3-pounder. Captain Wynne's Troop of yeomanry will join you on Monday at the Black Bull to replace the Kells Corps, which will proceed to Kells.

You are to proceed with the Force under your command, in the margin stated, towards Tara Hill, where it is reported numbers of the rebels are assembled in great disorder. When you have effected the immediate object of the service you are sent upon, you will fall back to the Black Bull, where your whole corps may be under cover, and act from thence as occasion may require, keeping up a communication with Lord Enniskillen on your right at Swords, Colonel Gordon on your left at Kilcock and also with Trim in your front.

You are to enforce to the officers and men under your command the necessity of maintaining the utmost regularity and good conduct that, though severity is requisite in punishing the insurgents, yet the peaceable inhabitants should feel security whenever the troops are in the neighbourhood. You will therefore strictly enjoin the soldiers not to burn houses or destroy property but such as you shall direct, and that no man is on any account to enter a house but by leave from his officer. You will represent to the inhabitants of the towns and villages you may pass through that inevitable destruction must be the consequence of a perseverance in their rebellious meetings, and that increased severity will be adopted by the troops in proportion to the time they persevere in their present conduct.

APPENDIX B

General Lake, feeling that many of the poor people have been deluded into their present situation by the artful suggestions of designing men, desires you will give encouragement to the inhabitants to return to their houses and assure them that they shall be protected if they deliver up their arms and manifest sincere contrition for their past conduct.

You will likewise hold out to the insurgents that the only hopes they have of pardon are by giving up their leaders and an unconditional surrender.

You will take particular care that the troops pay the value of the provisions they may purchase from the peaceable inhabitants.

(Signed) G. HAVITT,
Adj.

Adjutant-General's Office
DUBLIN, *May 27th,* 1798

APPENDIX C

Marshal Beresford

Sir,   10*th November*, 1813

    Agreeable to your Excellency's desire expressed in Lt. Col. Hope's letter of yesterday to Lt. Col. Bradford, I do myself the honour to inform you that, according to the instructions I had previously received from Major-General Murray, Q.M.G., the Fourth Division, having assembled at Daybreak on the morning of the 10th inst., upon the ground of encampment of General Giron's Corps, and having driven in the enemy's piquets, Lt. Col. Ross's troop of Horse Artillery and Major Sympkins' and Captain Douglas' Brigades of nine-pounders under the command of Lt. Col. Frazer opened about 7 A.M. a well-directed fire on the enemy's right Redoubt, which covered the village of Sava, covering the approach of the Provisional Battalion in Major-General Anson's Brigade and commanded by Colonel Bingham, which was directed to storm and carry it. After a short cannonade the enemy abandoned the Redoubt on the advance of our troops to attack.

    I then directed Major-General Anson, supported by the Portuguese (under the command of Colonel Vasconcellos), to attack the village, which the enemy still held against General Giron's Spanish corps. Which they effected with little loss and continued their progress and carried the enemy's camp of huts upon the brown detached height in rear of the village, Major-General Ross's Brigade, which was kept in reserve, following from the height on which the Redoubt was to the village as the other two Brigades advanced.

    Having halted and collected the Division in rear of this height, I directed Major-General Anson to co-operate

APPENDIX C

with the 7th Division in the attack of the Redoubt in the enemy's position in front of that Division, whilst Colonel Vasconcellos with the Portuguese Brigade moved a little more to the left, where the position recedes and where the slopes are wooded up to the top.

The enemy was driven out and the Redoubt carried by the 40th and 48th regiments, the former commanded by Lt. Col. Thornton and the latter by Brevet Major Bell. Here I halted and collected the Division as directed by the previous instructions already alluded to from Major-General Murray, the enemy being in considerable force and apparently inclined to defend a ridge which crosses the ridge we occupied and which leads from a long, heathy height to the village of St. Pé and on which they had erected a very strong redoubt.

I was directed by his Excellency the Commander-in-Chief, who had witnessed all our previous attacks, to attack and drive them from it. This was executed by the Portuguese Brigade, the enemy retiring across the Nivelle by the village of St. Pé and the bridges between that and the village of Ascain. We followed to a height over the river and between those villages, where we halted for the night. The retreat of the enemy's troops which occupied the Redoubt being cut off by this movement, they surrendered to Lt. Col. Colborne of the Light Division.

The conduct of the Division was such as I could desire. To Major-Generals Anson and Ross and Colonel Vasconcellos I feel much indebted, and my thanks are due to Lt. Col. Frazer and the three Brigades of guns under the command of Lt. Col. Ross, Major Sympkins and Captain Douglas for their conduct against the enemy's first Redoubt.

From the comparative lightness of the guns and the extreme badness of the roads, which delayed the progress of the nine-pounders against the enemy's position afterwards, Lt. Col. Ross's Brigade was enabled to afford me more effectual assistance, but it is impossible for any officer to be more attentive and zealous than Major

Sympkins is at all times or one who under every circumstance has his Brigade in better order. The conduct of the 40th and 48th Regiments commanded by Lt. Col. Thornton and Bt. Major Bell in the attack of the enemy's Redoubt in their position was conspicuous. I likewise feel much indebted to Colonel Bingham, Provisional Battalion, Lt. Col. Maclean, 27th Regiment, and Bt. Major Thomas in command of the Light Companies. The Portuguese Brigade as usual conducted itself to my satisfaction, particularly the Caçadores under the command of Major Lillie in the attack of the village of Saran. Major-Gen. Ross's Brigade, having been kept in reserve, was not employed. To my Divisional and Personal Staff I am at all times indebted for their zeal and gallantry and on no occasion more than on the present.

To His Excellency, Marshal Sir W. C. Beresford.

(Signed) G. L. COLE

INDEX

Abercromby, Sir Ralph, 16, 17, 22
American Wars, 110-111, 128, 130, 132

Belmore, Lord, Lowry Cole's grandfather, 2
Beresford, Marshal, 69-70, 71-74, 76, 77, 101, 102, 104
Bingham, Sir George, description of Napoleon at St. Helena, 160-163
Blücher, 119-120, 125, 127, 129, 149
Bowles, George, 81-83
—— Capt. William, 128, 130, 149, 186

Cole, Arthur, 11-12, 20, 23-25, 29, 31-32, 52-53, 210-212
—— Lady Elizabeth Anne (Lady Elizabeth Magenis), 12, 29, 126
—— Lady Florence (Lady Florence Balfour), 12, 30
—— Lady Frances (Lady Frances Harris), 36, 37, 111, 116, 117, 118; engagement and marriage to Lowry Cole, 137-144; her dairy, 155, 160, 164; description of Paris after the Restoration, 174-178; draughtswoman and gardener, 182-184; birth of a daughter, 185-186; birth of a son, 188, 189, 198; her description of Mauritius, 204-206, 207-209, 210, 233, 234, 242
—— Galbraith Lowry, The Hon. Sir, ancestry, 1-2; birth, 4-5; education and military training, 5; at Stuttgart, 8; beginning of military career, 10-11; at Vinegar Hill, 13; returned for County Fermanagh, 13-14; Lieut.-Colonel in General Villette's regiment, 18; diary in Alexandria, 18-19; attachment to Lady Kitty Pakenham, 27, 28, 30, 36, 110; attachment to Lady Frances Harris, 36, 37, 111; command of Inniskillings, 40; at Maida, 45 - 50; promoted Major-General, 51; on Sir Arthur Wellesley's staff in Spain, 52, 54; first experiences in the Peninsula, 54-67; relations with Wellington, 60; incidents in lines of Torres Vedras, 64-68; description of Albuera, 70-78; wounded at Salamanca, 84, 85, 86, 92; suffering of troops on retreat into Portugal, 88-89; description of Spanish life and people, 90-91; K.C.B. conferred, 93-94; Battle of Vittoria, 96-97; Battles of the Pyrenees, 96-108; at Bordeaux, 105; return to Ireland, 109-110; public thanks given to, in the House, 111-112; promoted to Northern Command, 134; relation with Fourth Division, 151; engagement and marriage to Lady Frances Harris, 137-144; character of, 141-142; regrets at missing Waterloo, 145, 147, 150; in Paris, 150-156; in command of the

Cole, Sir G. L.—*continued*
Reserves, 151, 158, 159, 166; command at Cambrai, 183; birth of children, 185, 189; Creevey's appreciation of, 188-189; life at Cambrai, 197-198; desire for home service, 198-199; governorships of Corfu and Ceylon refused, 199-200; offer of peerage refused, 202; made Governor of Mauritius, 202; description of Mauritius, 204-209; official attitude in Mauritius, 213-215, 222-223; attitude to slavery (*see* under Slavery); and Dr. Slater, 215-217; Governorship of Cape Colony accepted, 231; American visitors, description of, 232-234; inspection tour in the Cape Colony, 235-242; "Sir Lowry's Pass," 242-245; leaves the Colony, 248; at Highfield Park, 250; appointed Colonel of Inniskilling Fusiliers, 251; death, 251
—— Lady Henrietta, "Rusty" (Lady Grantham), 12-13, 26, 28, 29, 30, 34-35, 36-37; marriage to Lord Grantham, 40-41, 152, 164, 166
—— John, Baron Mount Florence, 2
—— Sir John, builder of Florence Court, 2
—— Lady Sarah (Lady Sarah Wynne), 12, 20, 35, 109
—— Lord. *See* 2nd Earl of Enniskillen
—— William, first settler, 1-2
—— William, Dean of Waterford, Lowry Cole's brother, 11-12, 20, 25, 31, 52-53
—— William Willoughby (Lowry Cole's father). *See* Lord Enniskillen
Colville, Sir Charles, 226, 227
Congress of Vienna, 130, 133

Cozens, Miss, 116, 165
Craig, Sir James, 41, 42
Crouch, Mrs., 6
Cradock, General, 54, 55
Creevey, Mr., 188

Dumaresq, Capt. Henry, 135, 205
Düring, Baron, 235, 239, 241, 242

Egyptian campaign, 15-20
Enniskillen, Lady (Lowry Cole's mother), 2, 27, 28
—— Lord (William), 1st Earl, 2, 3, 4, 5, 6, 13, 28-29
—— John, Lord, 2nd Earl (earlier Viscount Cole), 5-10, 20, 21, 25, 27, 28, 34; marriage, 51; letters to, 75, 87, 102, 111

Fitzherbert, Mrs., 6-7, 9, 21
Fouché, 168, 169, 171, 173, 177
Fourth Division, The, 96, 97, 98, 99, 100, 102, 104, 105, 112, 135

Goderich, Lord (the Hon. Frederick Robinson), 91-92, 112, 116, 165, 166-167, 180, 222, 225, 231
Grantham, Lord, marriage to Lady Henrietta Cole, 41, 43, 61, 147, 149, 152, 153, 154, 155, 164
Grouchy, Irish landing, 33-34

Harris, Lady Catherine (Lady Catherine Bell), 116, 117, 119, 139, 232, 234
—— Lady Frances. *See* Lady Frances Cole
Hely-Hutchinson, General, 17, 18, 22
Hertford, Lady, description of her ball, 126-128

Inniskilling Fusiliers, 27, 40, 45, 111, 125, 251

INDEX

de Lacey, General Maurice, 42
Louis XVIII., 112, 113-114; in England, 121-124; in Brussels, 131-132, 150-151, 168-170, 172-173, 178
Lowe, Sir Hudson, 162, 223, 224-225

Maida, battle of, 44-50
Malmesbury, Lady, 5; correspondence with Lord Cole, 6-10, 115-116, 117, 139, 140, 156; in Paris, 164-170, 178, 179-189; at Cambrai, 194-197
—— Lord, 5-6, 8, 116, 200-201, 202
Marmont, General, 43, 83, 84, 92
Masséna, 62, 63, 68, 79, 89
Mauritius, 202-228
Moore, Sir John, 16, 50, 51, 54, 60, 88
Murat (King Joachim), 50, 51, 131

Napoleon, Egyptian campaign, 15, 18; makes peace with England, 20; crowned Emperor, 37-38, 39, 51, 54, 101; Elba, 112; escape and the Hundred Days, 130-134, 135, 142; surrender, 154; Sir George Bingham's description of, at St. Helena, 160-163, 170-171, 172, 223, 229
Nelson, 38-39

Orange, Prince of, 126, 127, 131, 132, 146; and Cape Colony, 229

Pakenham, Sir Edward, 110, 134

Pakenham, Lady Kitty, Duchess of Wellington, 27, 28, 30, 36, 110
Paris, Peace of, 106, 112
—— after the Restoration, 164-181
Pyrenees, battles of, 96-105

Robinson, the Hon. Frederick. *See* Lord Goderich
—— the Hon. Mrs., 36, 81, 118, 119, 120; description of Lady Hertford's ball, 126-128, 129; account of the Field of Waterloo, 147-148
Roverea, Major, 45, 57-58, 59, 66, 67, 70-72, 77, 96, 98
Russia, Emperor Alexander of, 124, 125, 127, 128-129, 153, 173

Salamanca, 82-87
Slavery, 7, 213, 217-220, 222, 245, 247
Smith, Sir Sydney, 15, 44
Soult, Marshal, 54-55, 70, 74-75, 86, 88, 96, 99, 101, 102, 106
Sweden, King of, 7-8

Villette, General, 17, 18

Waterloo, battle of, and after, 145-146, 147-163
Wellesley, Sir Arthur, Duke of Wellington, 49; supreme control as General Wellesley, 55; as Lord Wellington, 60, 62, 76, 79-80; at Salamanca, 81-84, 85; in Madrid, 87, 90; in London, 92, 95, 97-102, 105, 107; in Paris, 148-149, 159, 173, 177; at Cambrai, 183, 184-185, 187, 189, 190-191; rumour of assassination of, 191, 192-194, 196-197, 201

THE END

Printed in Great Britain by R. & R. CLARK, LIMITED, *Edinburgh.*

www.ingramcontent.com/pod-product-compliance
Lightning Source LLC
Chambersburg PA
CBHW032125160426
43197CB00008B/524